Kolonie-Deutsch

A Bur Oak Book

Kolonie-Deutsch
Life and Language in Amana

An Expanded Edition
PHILIP E. WEBBER

University of Iowa Press · Iowa City

University of Iowa Press, Iowa City 52242
www.uiowapress.org
Copyright © 1993 by Iowa State University Press
First University of Iowa Press edition, 2009
Printed in the United States of America

The University of Iowa Press is a member of Green Press
Initiative and is committed to preserving natural resources.

Printed on acid-free paper

Library of Congress Cataloging-in-Publication Data
Webber, Philip E., 1944–
Kolonie-Deutsch: life and language in Amana /
by Philip E. Webber.—An expanded ed.
p. cm.—(A Bur Oak book)
Includes bibliographical references and index.
ISBN-13: 978-1-58729-830-1 (pbk.)
ISBN-10: 1-58729-830-9 (pbk.)
1. Amana Society—History. 2. German language—
Dialects—Iowa. I. Title.
HX656.A4W43 1993
977.7'653—dc22   2009011111

For my wife, Janice, and my sister Mary

Each has, in her own way, helped me to cherish
the legacy of my German-speaking parents

CONTENTS

PREFACE

I OWA'S AMANA COLONIES represent the last enclave of German Pietists known as the Community of True Inspiration. Residents of the Colonies practiced a form of theocratic communitarianism from the mid-1800s until 1932, when this traditionally closed sectarian society opened itself to greater contact with the outside world by adopting a dual system of secular and church governance.

Both before and after the Change of 1932, local speakers of German exhibited unusual tenacity in language maintenance. Amana German (or Kolonie-Deutsch) developed characteristic forms of grammar and pronunciation, and even individual microdialects in each of the seven constituent villages. While several specialized and fairly technical studies have been done on the language itself, the present volume is the first broad-based sociolinguistic study on patterns of language use and attitudes toward language and ethnicity in the Amana Colonies.

As in previous studies, I have relied heavily upon direct interviews (with some fifty individuals), allowing sources to speak from their own perspectives and thereby bring alive the account of language use as an indicator of evolving social patterns and values in the Amana Colonies. Every attempt has been made to evoke the drama of life in the colonies through a general ethnographic approach in which language study is the focus, rather than the exclusive goal, of the investigation.

Kolonie-Deutsch presents basic information on language and culture in the Amana Colonies, while frequently signaling possibilities for further research by scholars in a variety of fields. Attention is called to recent studies and other investigations in progress. The volume concludes with the fullest single bibliography available on life in the Amana Colonies.

PHILIP E. WEBBER

ACKNOWLEDGMENTS

ALTHOUGH I BEGAN doing fieldwork in the Amana Colonies in the late 1970s, my first systematic interviews were conducted in 1981 as a Mellon Fellow participating in the University of Iowa's University House Program (now the University of Iowa Center for Advanced Studies). This work resulted in several presentations at professional conferences but was forced to await serious follow-up until 1988, when a grant from the Iowa Humanities Board/National Endowment for the Humanities to the Museum of Amana History allowed me to serve as chief humanist for the project of compiling an archive of taped samples of Amana German. In this undertaking, Lanny Haldy, Director of the Museum, and Barbara S. Hoehnle, Librarian at the Museum, provided excellent administrative support and numerous useful suggestions. The grant was renewed, and the work sponsored by it culminated with the public inauguration of the tape archive in 1990. Part of a sabbatical leave from Central College in 1990 was devoted to the analysis of data from the taped material.

While I conducted most of the interviews myself, Emilie Hoppe, Barbara S. Hoehnle, Peter Hoehnle, and Gaycia Neubauer deserve a word of hearty thanks for their voluntary efforts in identifying and taping several key sources. Quite clearly, those to whom I owe the greatest debt of gratitude are the dozens of individuals who allowed themselves to be recorded individually or in small groups.

Valuable insights were gained into the earliest period of Amana's history through my work as the Germanist on a team that catalogued the correspondence of Christian Metz under a grant in 1992 to the Museum of Amana History from the Historical Resource Development Program of the State Historical Society of Iowa. I appreciate the opportunities for research and contact with specialists in other fields made possible by the work on this project.

I also wish to acknowledge all whose criticism of the manuscript in its development have improved the final product: Carol De Vore, Aulton Durham, Lanny Haldy, Barbara S. Hoehnle, Jason Houghton, Lawrence L. Rettig, and Janice E. Webber.

Finally, my thanks to the following organizations for their generous support of *Kolonie-Deutsch:* the Amana Heritage Society, the Amana Preservation Foundation, the Amana Arts Guild, the Amana Church Society, the Amana Society, and Central College.

ACKNOWLEDGMENTS FOR THE PAPERBACK EDITION

I OWE A DEBT of gratitude to many residents of the Amana Colonies who have encouraged me and offered their continuing friendship. Some, such as the late Lina Unglenk and Arthur W. (Artie) Selzer, can be thanked only through an expression of cherished memories. Others, such as Erna Fels, deserved more acknowledgment in the first edition. Many, including Barbara S. Hoehnle, may not even suspect how much they have helped me. The list of persons whom I might mention is long. I have tried to do what I believe is most appropriate in Amana itself by offering private but sincere thanks to individuals and credit for any success that my work may enjoy to the larger Amana community.

Nevertheless, two individuals deserve specific mention not only for help, but also because of what they represent: Lanny Haldy and Peter Hoehnle.

No investigator of Amana history and culture can afford to bypass the Amana Heritage Museum and its resources, particularly its library. It is Lanny Haldy, executive director of the Amana Heritage Society, who enabled us to make a selection of photographic material for this edition, including several photos that have not previously enjoyed the attention they deserve. The Museum reflects the energy and vision of Lanny and his staff. In thanking him, I am also thanking the Amana Heritage Society.

Peter Hoehnle, still young in his career, is already an established scholar of Amana history. In thanking him for his support, I am also expressing confidence in the potential of future scholarship (by both Peter Hoehnle and others) to help us understand more fully the wonder that was and is Amana.

At Central College, Jane Friedman's assistance was invaluable. My greatest inspiration, however, has always been and remains that of my wife, Jan.

INTRODUCTION TO THE
PAPERBACK EDITION

S INCE PUBLICATION of *Kolonie-Deutsch* in 1993, Amana has
witnessed a host of developments that make it an even more intriguing destination for both casual visitors and serious investigators. This
new prefatory chapter sets out to help visitors plan an up-to-date itinerary
for an informed exploration of the Amana Colonies. At the same time, both
general and specialized research on Amana has continued at a brisk pace;
the following short bibliographic essay will help readers pursue those topics
that they find compelling. Finally, there remains a great deal of research to
do, particularly on the language; we hope that this new paperback edition
of Kolonie-Deutsch can stimulate such research.

There is no better place to make an acquaintance with the Amana
Colonies than at the Amana Heritage Museum. For those who do not live
in the vicinity, a visit to the website at http://www.amanaheritage.org is
a wonderful place to begin, with links to information on special events,
exhibits, general and archival collections, heritage sites, and the museum's
bookstore. There is also a link to the Iowa Heritage Digital Collections,
containing some three hundred digitized images (including newspaper
clippings and maps) documenting Amana's history.

The Museum Bookstore offers a representative sampling of literature on the Amana Colonies published since the first edition of this book.
Although the following paragraphs introduce a few older or less widely
disseminated studies, the majority—and certainly most of those considered
foundational for a study of Amana's history and culture—are available via
the bookstore. The online catalog provides insightful summaries of the
contents of books offered for sale and thereby suggests in some detail just
what one might expect to encounter in a study of the Amana Colonies. It is
noteworthy that the bookstore offers back issues of journals with germane
articles for the study of Amana history, as well as earlier imprints such as
Lawrence Rettig's *Amana Today*—cited in the original *Kolonie-Deutsch*

bibliography—with its rich collection of primary sources documenting the events leading up to and following the Great Change from a communal to a free enterprise system in 1932.

For research prior to taking a trip to the Amanas—whether a first encounter or the latest in a series of visits—one can scarcely do better than to consult the National Register of Historic Places Travel Itinerary, with contextual essays on the Colonies by the Amana Heritage Society's executive director, Lanny Haldy. The Amana Colonies Convention and Visitors Bureau provides a guide currently entitled *Amana Colonies: The Handcrafted Escape* that can be ordered or downloaded from the internet. The bureau and the Amana Heritage Society have collaborated in producing *Amana Colonies by Car*, a CD that allows visitors to get a solid overview of the area while driving at a personally comfortable pace. Maps are available for walking tours of Amana and Middle Amana. The newspaper *Willkommen* continues to provide information on a variety of opportunities for visitors.

My recommendation is that, if seasonal opening times permit, the visitor should first make the loop of sites shown on the front of the Amana Heritage Society's *Amana Heritage Sites*. This self-paced tour begins in the village of Amana with the Amana Heritage Museum, where—in addition to the must-see regular and special exhibits—visitors can enjoy a video that provides excellent background on the Colonies' history and heritage. The loop continues through the intact Communal Kitchen and Cooper Shop in Middle Amana, to the High Amana General Store, the Communal Agricultural Museum in South Amana, the Amana Community Church in Homestead, the Homestead Store Museum with its exhibits of craft and industry products, and the Homestead Blacksmith Shop.

Tours are also available for bikers, hikers, and adventurers who wish to use either their own Global Positioning System device or one checked out at the Amana Heritage Museum. The annual cycle of events includes—to name but a few featured activities—an Easter egg hunt for children, craft demonstrations, industrial tours, wine tours, a barn tour, and a glimpse of Amana's Christmas past.

A particularly accessible gateway to any culture is its culinary heritage, and there is an abundance of cookbooks for those who wish to bring a taste of the Colonies into their own kitchens. Emilie Hoppe and Rachel Ehrman's *Seasons of Plenty* explains the traditional foodways of the Colonies as a reflection of their yearly cycle of work, celebration, and day-to-day life. Also worth considering are the Amana Heritage Society and the Amana Preservation Foundation's *Guten Appetit from Amana Kitchens* and Sue

Goree and Joan Bourret's *German Recipes: Old World Specialties and Photography from the Amana Colonies*, to name but two other cookbooks.

The Amana Arts Guild deserves recognition for fostering the tradition of fine handwork that continues in the Colonies to the present day. The guild's Art and Craft Series offers a stimulating overview of this legacy of Amana culture. Among newer titles in the series are Rene Driscoll's *Knitting of the Amana Colonies*, Emilie Hoppe's *Craftwork for the Kitchens and Gardens of the Amana Colonies*, Emilie Hoppe and Gordon Kellenberger's *Hooked Rugs of the Amana Colonies*, Gordon Kellenberger's *Pottery of the Amana Colonies*, Gordon Kellenberger and Barbara Hoehnle's *Blacksmithing of the Amana Colonies*, and Renate Schulte's *Calico Prints of the Amana Colonies*. Marjorie Albers, already an established author with a special interest in the furniture of the Colonies, collaborated with Peter Hoehnle to produce *Amana Style Furniture, Arts, Crafts, Architecture, and Gardens*. There is also continuing interest in Amana's tradition of fine lithography. Emilie Hoppe and Gordon Kellenberger's *Lithography of the Amana Colonies* is a good place to begin, along with Amy Worthen's catalog for a landmark exhibition at the Des Moines Art Center, *Fruits and Flowers Carefully Drawn from Nature*. Another exhibition with a catalog that merits attention (*Inspiration and Translation* by James White, et al.) was held at Carnegie Mellon University's Hunt Institute for Botanical Documentation. Lanny Haldy's essay in that catalog has a subtitle that summarizes so much about the place of lithography and other media of visual expression in the colonies: "Art for the Sake of the Community."

The last few years have witnessed a gratifying increase in research on the natural and built environments of the Amana Colonies. A compact but excellent overview is Gordon and Jean Kellenberger's *Architecture of the Amana Colonies*. Iowa's many barn enthusiasts will welcome Deb Schense and Carolyn Haase's *Eastern Iowa's Historic Barns and Other Farm Structures*. Although less likely to be accessed by the casual reader, Evan Lafer's *Barns and Communal Agricultural Buildings of the Amana Colonies* contains material that the specialist will not wish to overlook. We hope that the information documented in the graduate theses of Brian Buttery, John Den Boer, and Richard DeLaurell will eventually be disseminated to broader audiences.

For those eager to immerse themselves in the study of Amana's traditional culture, Joan Liffring-Zug Bourret, John Zug, Allyn Neubauer, Don Shoup, and others offer a variety of highly readable and informative monographs. Because most of us approach the Colonies as outsiders, it is worth considering how Amana has been portrayed over time in various published accounts and just what we expect to find when we arrive at our destination. Lanny Haldy's "In All the Papers," Joan Bourret and Dorothy Crum's *Life in Amana*, and Michelle Smith's "Painting the Living Scenery of Amana" deal with the media portrayal of the Amanas. While these studies focus on the outsider's portrayal of the Colonies during earlier eras, they are by no means without relevance—or caveat—for today's visitors to the Amana Colonies and other historic communal sites.

It is probably fair to say that most of us will arrive in Amana with camera in hand. The desire for memorable images can also be satisfied through a number of high-quality resources replete with images that document the Colonies' history. Abigail Foerstner's *Picturing Utopia*, now available in paperback, and Joan Bourret's *The Amanas: A Photographic Journey*, the Amana Heritage Society's video *Amana, the Community of True Inspiration*, and the Iowa Heritage Digital Collections help casual visitors and serious scholars alike to probe Amana's communal- and post-communal eras. Although no longer available, the Amana Heritage Society Calendar provided a fine selection of high-quality reproductions of historic photos.

Another source of insight into Amana's history consists of personal memoirs. The second edition of Barbara Yambura and Eunice Bodine's *A Change and a Parting: My Story of Amana* is perhaps the most familiar example. For variety of perspectives, one can turn to the collections that Robert Wolf has put together. These vignettes, many developed at Free River Press writing workshops, include memories and anecdotes by Marie Calihan, Rachel Ehrman, Mary Ann Fels, Barbara Hoehnle, Charles Hoehnle, Emilie Hoppe, Marietta Moershel, Roy Moser, Gaycia Neubauer, Dianne Rathje, and Lawrence Rettig. On my own bookshelf, I reserve a special place for the childhood recollections of Henrietta M. Ruff and Glenn H. and Guy Wendler, who experienced life in the Colonies as remembered today by relatively few. The late Marie L. Selzer's *Hobelspaen*, cited in the first edition of this work, is once again available thanks to her grandson Peter Hoehnle's generous sharing of a cache of the books.

As I am completing the text of this introductory chapter, the second round of the Kolonie Kinder project is under way. With the involvement of the Amana Arts Guild and others, recollections of the Colonies' oldest residents are being collected for eventual publication in a book for children (and, I would presume, for all of us who are still young at heart). Stories may be shared on a broad range of topics, in either English or German.

The *sine qua non* of Amana's communal society was, of course, its dedication to the Inspirationist faith. The writings of Peter Hoehnle offer a broad understanding of this faith-centered community and how it functioned.

Janet W. Zuber has continued to translate foundational documents of this tradition, including Johann Friedrich Rock's autobiographical writings and the Inspirationist *Profession of Faith*. Zuber's attractive anthology *The Morning Star*, which gathers a rich selection of Inspirationist testimonies from 1715 through 1883, is a unique collection of primary sources translated by Zuber into English. All of these works are part of the impressive corpus of work by Janet W. Zuber (see citations in the earlier edition of *Kolonie-Deutsch*) that won her the Communal Studies Association's 2007 Distinguished Scholar award.

It was a pleasant surprise to learn that Lanny Haldy had compiled a list of Inspirationist imprints from Ebenezer (outside Buffalo, New York, and site of the first Inspirationist settlement in North America) and Amana. Fortunately, this resource was published in time to be cited in the recommended readings list following this introduction.

It is hard to overestimate the importance of the publication of F. Alan DuVal and Peter Hoehnle's updated study of Amana's charismatic founding leader, Christian Metz (1793–1867). Jonathan Andelson and I have also published studies that enrich our understanding of Metz. A unique gift by Marietta Moershel and her family in memory of Carl F. Moershel, a Metz descendant, has placed a rich collection of Metz letters and journals in the Museum of Amana History, and one can only guess the importance that this corpus of material will have for future research.

A true milestone for the Amana church today is the translation and publication of the *Catechized Instruction Concerning the Teachings on Salvation*. This is the first statement of its sort in English for the members of the Community of True Inspiration. There are currently approximately 375 adult members, plus a considerable roll of Sunday School attendees.

Only two of the lay elders who were serving when *Kolonie-Deutsch* first appeared are still active. A full contingent consists of some ten to twelve elders, of which four are currently female. Services continue to feature some scripture, hymns, and prayers in German, but the dominant language is clearly English. The last elder to regularly offer a full service primarily in German was the late Henry Schiff (1903–1995). Since then, a full service in German has been held only for the outside audience of a German Studies Association conference. Meanwhile, the church building in the village of Amana (known locally as Main Amana) has been renovated with a fellowship hall added. All services are now recorded, and weekly worship is conducted at local care facilities.

A perennially intriguing aspect of life in communal societies is the way work is allocated and carried out. The most recent study on this topic is

Angela Tjaden's research on the use of hired labor during the communal era. Lawrence Rettig's "Work in the Amana Colonies" is an essay that deserves to be published in a form that will reach a broader readership. For more detailed research, the reader is referred to Peter Hoehnle's studies, especially "Common Labor, Common Lives," "Community in Transition," and "Machine in the Garden."

There is also an increase in literature on Amana for younger readers. Author Ann Heinrichs and illustrator Matt Kania (who have collaborated on a number of volumes devoted to various states) present the Amana Colonies in an attractive children's hardback devoted to Iowa. The Amana Folklife Curriculum of Caroline Trumpold and Gordon Kellenberger's *Time and Tradition* presents activities planned primarily to coincide with holidays in the school calendar. These activities compare and contrast current practices with those of earlier generations. The Amana Heritage Society Traveling Trunk, available to elementary and middle school educators doing a unit on Amana history, presents realia that bring alive Amana's rich cultural and historical legacy. The gold standard, however, remains the communal societies field trip to the Amana Heritage Museum, where children assume the roles of members of a communal society. The Amana Arts Guild also offers a traveling trunk that focuses on the Colonies' historical and ongoing tradition of fine crafts.

If I might make one plea it would be that the material collected by Millie Frese and Emilie Hoppe in a special "Visiting the Amanas" edition of *The Goldfinch* be reissued. This special volume includes short and highly readable articles that treat the Amana Colonies' history and German heritage; the confusion between the residents of the Amanas and the Amish; education in earlier years; baseball, games, and rhymes; craft traditions; and much more. Some of the material has been subsequently used by other authors, but an updated version of this collection would nevertheless be a contribution to the young reader's bookshelf.

For readers with more background and literacy skills, Paul Marx's *Utopia in America* and Thomas Streissguth's *Utopian Visionaries* point to an upsurge of interest in utopian and communal societies. Robert S. Fogarty brought out a new edition of Charles Nordhoff's landmark *American Utopias*; Brian Berry, Gregory Claeys and Lyman Sargent, Donald Pitzer, and Robert Sutton have all produced works that enrich our understanding of such communities. The Office of Cultural Resource Management of the U.S. Department of the Interior's National Park Service has created an online resource titled *Preserving America's Utopian Dream*. The National Register of Historic Places Travel Itinerary for the Amana Colonies at http://www.nps.gov/history/nr/travel/amana provides not only an excellent introduction to the Colonies themselves, but also foundational background information on utopian societies in the United States. The online bibliographies of communal studies offered by the Luther College library at http://library.luther.edu/pages/csabibsz.htm and by the Communal Studies Association at http://www.communalstudies.info/bibliographies.shtml will serve the scholar who wishes to probe deeper. We hope that a successor to the Communal Studies Association's handy foldout *Guide to Historic Communal Sites in the United States* will appear.

Even among recent publications that clearly focus on Amana, there are recurring references to the Colonies' place in the broader context of America's communal and utopian societies. Examples of this are the frequently comparative studies of Jonathan Andelson and Peter Hoehnle. Scholars of religious and social experiments who have been unable to secure a copy of the 1891 *History of the Amana Society, or Community of True Inspiration* by William Perkins and Barthinius Wick can now enjoy a reprint edition indexed by Don Heinrich Tolzmann.

Research for the first edition of this book began with taped interviews of speakers of Amana German (Kolonie-Deutsch) so it is appropriate that this new prefatory chapter conclude with an overview of expanded opportunities for scholars of the language itself. At the end of *Kolonie-Deutsch* I stated that "at some point in the [twenty-first] century, the last speaker to have acquired Kolonie-Deutsch as the naturally transmitted, preferred language will pass from the scene." It was awkward for me and deeply disturbing for Amana residents to have this misinterpreted as a prediction that all speakers of Kolonie-Deutsch would have expired by the beginning of the year 2000. Earlier this year, a speaker in the prime of life gently reminded me that he is indeed alive, well, and able to communicate in Kolonie-Deutsch. For this I am very glad. Still, researchers wishing to work with human sources need to bear in mind that speakers available for interviews are becoming ever fewer. There is enough work remaining to be done that there need not be turf battles among investigators, least of all between the author of this book and those who may follow.

Much of my own work has consisted of descriptive sociolinguistics, and I would welcome deeper probing of the language itself, or an attempt to see how the use and status of the language has changed during the past decade and a half. Which sounds, forms, sentence patterns, and vocabulary of Kolonie-Deutsch remain fairly intact, and which appear to reflect a pattern of decay or shift? Which situations still prompt spontaneous use of the language, and by which groups of speakers? Possibilities abound for individuals at virtually every stage of their training and research program.

The earliest extant recordings of the language were made in 1934 by University of Iowa's Professor Erich Funke (1891–1974) on aluminum disks. The "Funke recordings," as they are sometimes called, have been given by Ruth Schmieder to the Amana Heritage Museum, where they have been digitized and await analysis. I have begun a modest study of Funke's work with these recordings.

Other interviews by myself and others have been digitized for eventual inclusion in "American Languages: Our Nation's Many Voices," http://digital.library.wisc.edu/1711.dl/AmerLangs. I am deeply indebted to Professor Mark L. Louden, University of Wisconsin, and the Max Kade Institute there, for accepting the Amana material as part of their very ambitious and uniquely worthwhile undertaking. While I was writing this new introduction, I received the digitized interviews and look forward to their eventual accessibility via the American Languages website. The Max Kade Institute at the University of Wisconsin has recently published the audio CD *German Words—American Voices Deutsche Wörter—Amerikanische Stimmen*, compiled and edited with a useful commentary by Mark L. Louden. The material was collected in various parts of the United States, and in some instances dates back to the 1940s. I sincerely hope that it will be possible to compile something similar for Amana German.

One need not be a professional researcher to support investigation into the scope and use of Amana German. Each bit of documentation—be it of sounds, sights, artifacts, or texts—represents something of personal worth whose value to a broader understanding of Amana's culture and history may only become evident at some future date. Individuals with access to speakers of Kolonie-Deutsch have an enviable opportunity to record these non-renewable resources. Recollections of personal experiences, lists of memorable vocabulary associated with the activities of daily life, anecdotes and humor, nature lore, and similar samples of authentic language can make a unique contribution to our understanding of life and language in Amana.

RECOMMENDED READINGS

Albers, Marjorie K., and Peter Hoehnle. *Amana Style Furniture, Arts, Crafts, Architecture, and Gardens.* Iowa City, Iowa: Penfield Books, 2005.

Allen, Anne B. "Amana Arts Guild: Preserving a Distinctive Heritage: In Amana,

Modern-Day Artists Are Reviving the Crafts of Their Ancestors." *The Iowan* 43.2 (1994): 20–23, 67.

Amana Arts Guild. http://www.amanaartsguild.com.

Amana Church Society. *Catechized Instruction Concerning the Teachings on Salvation Presented in Accordance to the Protestant Apostles' Understanding of the Holy Scriptures of the Spirit of God to the Blessed Use of the Members of the Community of True Inspiration.* Part II. transl. Henry J. Ruff. Amana, Iowa: Amana Church Society, 1999.

_____, and Janet W. Zuber. *Glaubensbekentniss = Profession of Faith.* Amana, Iowa: Amana Church Society, 1988.

Amana Colonies Convention and Visitors Bureau. http://www.amanacolonies. com.

_____. *Amana Colonies: The Handcrafted Escape.* Annual publication also accessible by download.

_____. *Willkommen: The Amana Colonies.* VHS. Amana, Iowa: Amana Colonies Convention and Visitors Bureau, 1992.

Amana Heritage Society. *Amana Heritage Sites: Visitor's Guide.* Foldout brochure.

_____. *Amana, the Community of True Inspiration.* VHS. Amana, Iowa: Amana Heritage Society and Stamats Film and Video, 1991.

_____. *Books about the Amana Colonies, German Heritage, and Communal Societies.* Amana, Iowa: Amana Heritage Society, 1996.

_____. *Calendar of the Amana Heritage Society* (earlier title: *The Perennial Calendar of the Amana Heritage Society*). Amana, Iowa: Amana Heritage Society, various years.

_____, and Amana Colonies Convention and Visitors Bureau. *Amana Colonies by Car: An Audio Driving Tour of the Seven Historic Amana Villages.* CD. Amana, Iowa: Amana Colonies Convention and Visitors Bureau, 2002.

_____, and Amana Preservation Foundation. *Guten Appetit from Amana Kitchens.* Deep River, Iowa: Brennan Printing, 2003.

Amana Society. *The Amana Colonies Featuring Seven Historic Villages.* Amana, Iowa: Amana Society, 1999.

_____. *Christmas Cookie Walk Collection.* Deep River, Iowa: Brennan Printing, 1995.

Andelson, Jonathan G. "The Community of True Inspiration from Germany to the Amana Colonies." In *America's Communal Utopias*, ed. Donald E. Pitzer. Chapel Hill, North Carolina: University of North Carolina Press, 1997. 181–203.

_____. "Introduction: Boundaries in Communal Amana." *Communal Societies* 14 (1994): 1–6.

_____. "Postcharismatic Authority in the Amana Society: The Legacy of Christian Metz." In *When Prophets Die: The Postcharismatic Fate of New Religious Movements*, ed. Timothy Miller. Albany: State University of New York Press, 1991. 29–45, 202–204.

_____. "What the Amana Inspirationists Were Reading." *Communal Societies* 14 (1994): 7–19.

Berry, Brian Joe Lobley. *America's Utopian Experiments: Communal Havens from Long-Wave Crises*. Hanover, New Hampshire: Dartmouth College, 1992.

Bjerklie, Steve. "The Amana Colonies: Mysticism and Common Sense." *Communities* 96 (1997): 58–59.

Bourret, Joan Liffring-Zug. *The Amanas: A Photographic Journey, 1959–1999*. Iowa City, Iowa: Penfield Press, 2000.

_____, and Dorothy Crum. *Life in Amana: Reporters' Views of the Communal Way, 1867–1935*. Iowa City, Iowa: Penfield Press, 1998.

_____, and John Zug. *The Amana Colonies, Seven Villages in Iowa: New World Home of the True Inspirationists*. Monticello, Iowa: Julin Printing, 1977.

Buttery, Brian Watson. "An Intervention in Story City, Iowa." Masters thesis, Iowa State University, 2004.

Claeys, Gregory, and Lyman Tower Sargent. *The Utopia Reader*. New York: New York University Press, 1999.

Communal Studies Association. Guide to Historic Communal Sites in the United States. http://www.communalstudies.info.

_____. "Making the Connection—Historic Communal Sites and Contemporary Communities." Program for Twenty-third Annual Conference of the Communal Studies Association, October 10, 11, 12, 1996.

Cosgel, Metin M. "Market Integration and Agricultural Efficiency in Communal Amana." *Communal Societies* 14 (1994): 36–48.

Decision Data, Inc. and Tallgrass Historians, L.C. *The Amana Colonies Historic Byway Inventory and Evaluation*. Ames, Iowa: Iowa Department of Transportation, 1998.

DeLaurell, Richard N. "Cartographic Representations of Community as Communication: A Case Study of the Amana Colonies." Ph.D. dissertation, University of Iowa, 1993.

Den Boer, John Benjamin. "Building Community: College Creek Cohousing." Masters thesis, Iowa State University, 2003.

Driscoll, Rene. *Knitting of the Amana Colonies*. Amana, Iowa: Amana Arts Guild, 1994.

DuVal, F. Alan, and Peter Hoehnle. *Christian Metz: German-American Religious Leader and Pioneer*. Iowa City, Iowa: Penfield Books, 2005.

Erickson, Lori. *Ghosts of the Amana Colonies*. Fort Madison, Iowa: Quixote Press, 1988.

Foerstner, Abigail. *Picturing Utopia: Bertha Shambaugh and the Amana Photographers*. Iowa City: University of Iowa Press, 2005.

Franklin-Weekley, Rachel. "Stewardship and Change in the Amana Colonies." *Preserving America's Utopian Dream. CRM* 24 (2001): 21–23. Available in CRM Online at the website of the U.S. Department of the Interior, National Park Service, http://crm.cr.nps.gov/issue.cfm?volume=24&number=09.

Frese, Millie K., and Emilie Hoppe, eds. Visiting the Amana Colonies, special issue. *The Goldfinch: Iowa History for Young People* 13.4 (April 1992).

Funke, Erich. Recordings of Amana Colonies Dialect by Prof. Erich Funke of the University of Iowa, 1934. CD. Housed at Museum of Amana History.

Goodwillie, Christian. "With Hands to Work and Hearts to God: America's Communal Utopias." *Early American Life* 36.2 (2005): 50–57.

Goree, Sue Roemig, and Joan Liffring-Zug Bourret. *German Recipes: Old World Specialties and Photography from the Amana Colonies*. Iowa City, Iowa: Penfield Books, 2002.

Grams, Kendra Ruth. "The Evolution of a New Spiritual Understanding in the Amana Church Society, 1855–2005." Bachelors thesis, Coe College, 2006.

Haldy, Lanny R. Contextual essays for "The Amana Colonies: A National Register of Historic Places Travel Itinerary of a Unique Historic Communal Society in Eastern Iowa." http://www.nps.gov/history/nr/travel/amana/index.htm.

_____. "In All the Papers: Newspaper Accounts of Communal Amana, 1867–1924." *Communal Societies* 14 (1994): 20–35.

_____. "Inspirationist Imprints in America, 1849–1929: A Bibliography of German-Language Books Produced by the Community of True Inspiration." *Communal Societies* 29 (2009): 69–88.

_____. "Joseph Prestele: Art for the Sake of the Community." In *Inspiration and Translation: Botanical and Horticultural Lithographs of Joseph Prestele and Sons*, ed. James J. White et al. Pittsburgh, Pennsylvania: Hunt Institute for Botanical Documentation, Carnegie Mellon University, 2005. 22–27.

Heinrichs, Ann, and Matt Kania. *Iowa*. Chanhassen, Minnesota: Child's World, 2006.

Hoehnle, Peter [Andrew]. *The Amana People: The History of a Religious Community*. Iowa City, Iowa: Penfield Books, 2003.

_____. "Carl Flick and Grant Wood: A Regionalist Friendship in Amana." *Iowa Heritage Illustrated* 82 (2001): 2–19.

_____. "Common Labor, Common Lives: The Social Construction of Work in Four Communal Societies, 1774–1932." Ph.D. dissertation, Iowa State University, 2003.

_____. "Communal Bonds: Contact between the Amana Society and Other Communal Groups, 1843–1932." *Communal Societies* 20 (2000): 59–90.

_____. "The Communal Wanderings of August Jacobi." *Communal Societies* 29 (2009): 41–52.

_____. "Community in Transition: Amana's Great Change 1931 to 1933." *Annals of Iowa* 60 (2001): 1–34.

_____. "The Great Change: The Reorganization of the Amana Society, 1931–1933." Master's thesis, Iowa State University, 1998.

_____. "Machine in the Garden: The Woolen Textile Industry of the Amana Society, 1785–1942." *Annals of Iowa* 61 (2002): 24–67.

_____. "A Short History of the Amana Society, 1714–2002." *Yearbook of German-American Studies* 37 (2002): 13–23.

_____. "With Malice toward None: The Inspirationist Response to the Civil War, 1860–1865." Bachelor's thesis, Cornell College, 1995.

_____. "With Malice toward None: The Inspirationist Response to the Civil War, 1860–1865." *Communal Societies* 18 (1998): 62–80.

Holl, Kristi. *Let Sleeping Ghosts Lie*. Unionville, New York: Royal Fireworks Press, 1999.

Hoppe, Emilie. *Craftwork for the Kitchens and Gardens of the Amana Colonies*. Amana, Iowa: Amana Arts Guild, 1991.

Hoppe, Emilie. "Life Is But a Pilgrimage." *Communities* 89 (1955): 51–53, 64.

_____, and Rachel Ehrman. *Seasons of Plenty: Amana Communal Cooking*. Iowa City: University of Iowa Press, 2006.

_____, and Gordon Kellenberger. *Hooked Rugs of the Amana Colonies*. Amana, Iowa: Amana Arts Guild, 1990.

_____, and Gordon Kellenberger. *Lithography of the Amana Colonies*. Amana, Iowa: Amana Arts Guild, 1993.

Kellenberger, Gordon. *Pottery of the Amana Colonies*. Amana, Iowa: Amana Arts Guild, 1992.

_____, and Barbara Hoehnle. *Blacksmithing of the Amana Colonies*. Amana, Iowa: Amana Arts Guild, 1988.

_____, and Jean Kellenberger. *Architecture of the Amana Colonies*. Amana, Iowa: Amana Arts Guild, 1987.

Kraus, George, E. Mae Fritz, and Helen Kraus. *The Story of an Amana Winemaker*. Iowa City, Iowa: Penfield Press, 1984.

Lafer, Evan L. *The Barns and Communal Agriculture Buildings of the Amana Colonies*. Prepared by National Trust for Historic Preservation, Midwest Office. Omaha, Nebraska: The Office, 1999.

Louden, Mark L. *German Words—American Voices Deutsche Wörter—Amerikanische Stimmen*. CD. Madison, Wisconsin: Max Kade Institute, 2007.

Madden, Etta M., and Martha L. Finch. *Eating in Eden: Food and American Utopias*. Lincoln: University of Nebraska Press, 2008.

Marx, Paul. *Utopia in America*. Evanston, Illinois: J. Gordon Burke, 2002.

National Park Service, Cultural Resource Management. *Preserving America's Utopian Dream*. CRM 24 (2001), http://crm.cr.nps.gov/issue.cfm?volume=24&number=09.

Neubauer, Allyn, Joan Liffring-Zug Bourret, and John Zug. *The Amana Colonies: Seven Historic Villages*. Monticello, Iowa: Julin Printing, 1993.

Nordhoff, Charles, and Robert S. Fogarty. *American Utopias*. Stockbridge, Massachusetts: Berkshire House, 1993.

Patterson, Maureen. *German Style Recipes from German-American Life*. Iowa City, Iowa: Penfield Books, 2005.

Perkins, William Robertson, Barthinius L. Wick, and Don Heinrich Tolzmann. *Amana: William Rufus Perkins' and Barthinius L. Wick's: History of the Amana Society, or Community of True Inspiration*. Bowie, Maryland: Heritage Books, 2000.

Pitzer, Donald E. *America's Communal Utopias*. Chapel Hill: University of North Carolina Press, 1997.

Rawls, Thomas H. "Iowa's Amana Colonies." *National Geographic Traveler* 12.4 (1995): 70–77.

Read, E. C .K., with photography by Greg Gillis. "On the Road to Amana: Meet the People, Taste the Good Food, and Discover the Fascinating History of Iowa's Famous Colonies." *Bon Appétit* 40.11 (1995): 164–168.

Rettig, Lawrence L. "Work in the Amana Colonies." In *Utopian Visions of Work and Community: A Collection of Essays from Presentations Sponsored by the National Endowment for the Humanities*, ed. Jay Semel and Annie Tremmel Wilcox. Iowa City: Obermann Center for Advanced Studies, University of Iowa, 1996. 85–92.

Rock, Johann Friedrich, and Janet W. Zuber. *The Humble Way: An Autobiographical Account of God's Guidance in the Life of Br. Johann Friedrich Rock*. Amana, Iowa: Amana Church Society, 1999.

_____, and Ulf-Michael Schneider. *Wie ihn Gott geführet und auf die Wege der Inspiration gebracht habe Autobiographische Schriften*. Leipzig: Evangelische Verlagsanstalt, 1999.

Roemig, Madeline. "The Individual and the Community: Education in Communal Amana." In *Communal Life: An International Perspective*, ed. Yosef Gorni, Iaácov Oved and Idit Paz. New Brunswick, New Jersey: Transaction Books, 1987. 317–323.

Ruff, Henrietta M. *Seasons to Remember: Recollections of an Amana Childhood*. Amana, Iowa: H. Ruff, 1996.

Schense, Deb M., and Carolyn Haase. *Eastern Iowa's Historic Barns and Other Farm Structures Including the Amana Colonies.* N.p.: Lulu.com, 2006.

Schulte, Renate. *Calico Prints of the Amana Colonies.* Amana, Iowa: Amana Arts Guild, 1989.

Shoup, Don, Joan Liffring-Zug Bourret, and John Zug. *The Amana Colonies.* Monticello, Iowa: Julin Printing Co, 1988.

Shumway, Pamela Heard. "Amana Governance Structures and Religious Beliefs." Ph.D. dissertation, George Mason University, 1995.

Simmons, John, and Eugene Williams. *Pioneer Spirit Sectarianism and Utopianism in the 19th Century.* Olathe, Kansas: RMI Media Productions, 1993.

Smith, Michelle C. "Painting the Living Scenery of Amana: A Case Study of Rhetoric Containment." *Communal Societies* 27 (2007): 27–46.

Society for German-American Studies. Program for Twenty-Sixth Annual Symposium of the Society for German-American Studies, 18–21 April 2002, Amana, Iowa.

Streissguth, Thomas. *Utopian Visionaries.* Minneapolis, Minnesota: Oliver Press, 1999.

Strohman, James. *Amana Colonies Guide to Dining, Lodging, and Tourism.* Ames: Iowa State University Press, 1997.

Sutton, Robert P. *Communal Utopias and the American Experience: Religious Communities, 1732–2000.* Westport, Connecticut: Praeger, 2003.

Tjaden, Angela. "The Communal System of the Amana Colonies: Impact of Hired Labor, 1884–1932." *Communal Societies* 29 (2009): 53–68.

Trumpold, Caroline, and Gordon Kellenberger. *Time and Tradition.* Amana, Iowa: Amana Arts Guild, 1990.

Trumpold, Cliff. *The Life and Times of the Amana Young Men's Bureau 1941–1969.* Amana, Iowa: Amana Heritage Society, 1995.

_____. *Now Pitching: Bill Zuber from Amana.* Middle, Iowa: Lakeside Press, 1992.

University of Iowa. Iowa Heritage Digital Collections. Amana Heritage Society. http://digital.lib.uiowa.edu/cdm4/browse.php?CISOROOT=%2Famana.

University of Wisconsin Digital Collections. American Languages: Our Nation's Many Voices. http://digital.library.wisc.edu/1711.dl/AmerLangs.

Webber, Philip E. "The Dreams of Christian Metz, Amana's Charismatic Founding Leader." *Communal Societies* 22 (2002): 9–25.

Wendler, Glenn H., and Guy H. Wendler. *The Commune's Last Child.* Sine loco: North Amana Workshops, 2005.

White, James J., Joseph Prestele, William Henry Prestele, Lugene B. Bruno, Susan H. Fugate, and Marcelee Konish. *Inspiration and Translation:*

Botanical and Horticultural Lithographs of Joseph Prestele and Sons. Pittsburgh, Pennsylvania: Hunt Institute for Botanical Documentation, Carnegie Mellon University, 2005.

Wolf, Robert, ed., illustrated by Bonnie Koloc. *An American Mosaic: Prose and Poetry by Everyday Folk.* New York: Oxford University Press, 1999.

Wolf, Robert. *Village Voices: Stories from the Amana Colonies.* Folk Literature Series. Lansing, Iowa: Free River Press, 1996.

Worthen, Amy N. *Fruits and Flowers Carefully Drawn from Nature: 19th Century Lithographs from the Amana Colonies.* Des Moines, Iowa: Des Moines Art Center, 2000.

Yambura, Barbara Selzer, and Eunice W. Bodine. *A Change and a Parting: My Story of Amana.* 2nd ed. Iowa City, Iowa: Penfield Press, 2001.

Zimmerman, Paul A., and Emma Zimmerman. *The History of Beer Brewing as Continued by the Community of True Inspiration in the "New World" at Ebenezer, New York, and in the Amana Colonies, Iowa.* Amana, Iowa: Amana Print Shop, 1982.

Zuber, Janet W. *The Morning Star: Words of Inspiration as Presented to the Community of True Inspiration.* Amana, Iowa: Amana Church Society, 2005.

Kolonie-Deutsch

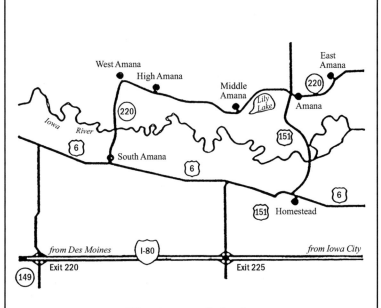

The Amana Colonies

1

An Introductory Overview

Willkommen!

EVEN THE MOST JADED TOURIST passing through Iowa can scarcely keep from taking special note of the Amana Colonies. At virtually any information station in the state, one can pick up an attractive brochure and map, published by the Amana Colonies Convention and Visitors Bureau, touting the well-nigh undisputed claim that the Colonies' seven historic villages are "Iowa's Leading Visitor Attraction." Eager travelers approaching the area on Interstate 80 are reminded by prominent signs that the Colonies are a National Historic Landmark, and all are warmly invited to stop at the Iowa Welcome Center, located on the northwest edge of the main village of Amana. Every indication, official or otherwise, seems to imply that to *really* see Iowa is to see the seven villages of the Amana Colonies.

What the seven villages have to offer is a community whose crafts, architecture, and institutions reflect and—to an extent—perpetuate the German heritage of earlier residents. For historical perspective, there is no better place to begin than the Museum of Amana History; for tips on current attractions, one is well advised to turn to the latest edition of the tabloid *Willkommen* (Welcome). In contrast to the expectations of many, the Amana Colonies are not and never have been an Amish settlement. Amana was founded in 1855 by Pietist adherents of the Community of True Inspiration who moved to Iowa under the leadership of Christian Metz.[1] A communal theocracy prevailed until the Great Change of 1932, when separate branches of governance were established for secular and religious matters. While few tourists want or expect too rigorous a dose of German-American culture, many are

3

delighted to be exposed to just enough to assure them that they have indeed seen the real thing.

Or perhaps more accurately many tourists crave the assurance that they have *heard* just a bit of the real thing! Quite a few older Colonists have a slight German accent, and in interview sessions a number of individuals related tales of zealous attempts, particularly in earlier years, at eradicating this indelible vestige of the mother tongue. The accent, however, is a familiar one in German-American circles and certainly poses no barriers to easy communication. The initial sound of the word *German* may resemble the consonant at the beginning of the word *chair*. For certain speakers, pronunciation of the consonant cluster [st] will occasionally be [št]. For example, the name of the village Homestead may sound as though it ought to be written *Homeshtead,* or even *Homeshtet,* and *store* may sound like *shtore.* A few older speakers pronounce *west* like *vest.* One often detects a slightly different coloring of certain vowels. The first vowel of *German* is typically pronounced with lips slightly rounded, and the patently non-German vowel of *pan* is often pronounced like that of *pen.* While outsiders may find these pronunciation patterns charming, one source noted with unmistakable bristle that she felt not at all complimented at being told by a visitor that she sounded just like Lawrence Welk, noting "der war frech da, gel?" (he was being fresh, don't you think?) and set to work in earnest to improve her English.

Some now realize, however, that in spiffing up their English they may have bypassed full development of their German. One Colonist lamented, "Ich hab' dann alsmal grad' ein bißl complex mit meinem German accent. Ich sage immer, ich kann nicht extra gut deutsch schwätzen und ich kann auch nicht extra gut englisch schwätzen. I'm right in between! [laughter]" (Sometimes I have just a bit of a complex about my German accent. I always say I can't speak especially good German, and I also can't speak especially good English. I'm right in between!) The situation is often one of classic schizoglossia, with the individual not securely in control of either language.

Other local residents assume a more pragmatic or even sanguine attitude. The proprietor of a business renowned in tourist circles for its quaint atmosphere confided in written communication that, as a matter of fact, her accent afforded her a distinct advantage: "If one has the German accent, visitors are more apt to consider [the speaker] a true member of the community, and that is often important to [tourists and customers]." It has even been hinted that, in some instances, mischievous Colonists with a bit of tongue-in-cheek humor have given enthusiastic but somewhat naive outsiders just a bit more than their money's worth of heavily accented "Amana English."

Visitors familiar with the German language are delighted to hear words such as *gel* and *net* (= *nicht wahr*) 'isn't that right?', or *Oma* 'Grandma' and *Opa* 'Grandpa' interjected into the local English. One grandmother reports being asked by her otherwise monolingual grandchild "*Oma*, are you *ufgeregt*" (i.e., *aufgeregt*) 'agitated, worked up'? Virtually every youngster knows that some of the grandparents' treasures are kept in the family *Schrank*, a large, upright clothes press used to hold a variety of items. Still other German terms for household furnishings and implements survive in the local English.

In instances where English and German have similar-sounding cognates, the English word may acquire a German semantic range, as in the remark by one Colonist that the local residents did not "stem from" any group of low social repute (cf. *stammen von* 'to originate from'). A worshiper returning from church might volunteer the information that a certain elder *held* (i.e., held services) that morning; like German *halten* 'to hold', the English verb 'to hold' is commonly used intransitively with the meaning 'to officiate'. Sometimes homonyms of the two languages do not even have similar meanings, but nevertheless lend themselves to bilingual wordplay, as in the roguish remark on a notably warm midsummer day that it was really getting to be hell outside (*hell* 'bright').

Even noncognate English words exhibit a usage pattern reminiscent of German: in local parlance, *once,* like German *einmal,* can mean either 'one time' or 'simply'. Hence, when a grandmother asked her grandchild to "get the mail once" (that is, simply go get the mail for her), the playful youngster, who was used to such German-influenced utterances, responded teasingly, "I'll do it this once, but don't ask me to do it again!" Asking someone if his or her child is *strange* does not necessarily constitute an insult: one is merely seeking to find out whether the youngster is shy (*fremd* 'strange, unfamiliar, shy').

Older Colonists recall overexact translations dating from earlier days when a sense for English idiom was imperfect, and examples of awkwardly literal renderings of German were commonplace. A resident whose first and preferred language is clearly German recalls wishing to stress the fact that she was due to take her turn, insisting that she was on the row (*an der Reihe sein* 'to have one's turn'). One poor chap is evidently still subject to teasing for having asked a family member what time he stood up that morning (*aufstehen* 'to arise from sleep, to wake up'). In sum, evidence abounds for those who crave palpable assurance that the German language was and is an essential part of the cultural legacy of the Amana Colonies.

The Three-Cornered Hat

SPEAKERS OF AMANA GERMAN are quick to point out that they are in fact prepared, as the situation and background of the speaker-partner may demand, to use any of three languages: American English, standard German, usually referred to as *Hochdeutsch* 'High German' or *Schriftdeutsch* 'German as it is written', and their own home-grown Amana German. The local variety of German is known by its speakers as *Kolonie-Deutsch,* a term usually pronounced with stress on the first vowel of the compound, deletion of the second vowel, and unrounding of the final diphthong, *Kólnie-Deitsch.*

As a sidelight, one might note that the pronunciation of *Kolonie* as a two-syllable word was probably established by the time that any living speakers learned the language. The evidence suggesting such a pronunciation comes from a humorous poem, composed in the earlier years of this century to celebrate the shenanigans of the communal-era night watchmen. The text from "Ein Gedankenspiel auf der Wachstube" refers at one point to the *Wachstube* 'watch-room' (actually, a watchtower) and laments that

> Auch ist unser Wächter system
> Ein hang-out für die excolonisten.
>
> ([The headquarters of] our watchmen's system is also
> a hang-out for the ex-Colonists.)

Apart from an occasional unaccented syllable at the beginning of a line, the scansion of this poem is quite regular, and remains so in the second line cited here only if one assumes, despite what may have been written, that *excolonisten* was intended to be read as *éx-col-nís-ten.* If the medial syllable had dropped out of *Kolonist,* it is reasonable to assume that the same process had taken place in *Kolonie.*

I asked a number of sources how they gauge the fluency of fellow speakers of Kolonie-Deutsch and found a striking degree of agreement in the responses offered. The genuine speaker appears to be an individual who can take a cue from a single word or two, switch to Kolonie-Deutsch, and then—as emphasized by several sources—continue speaking the language in complete sentences. I also found that there seemed to be some feeling that a true speaker of Amana German could keep several conversations running simultaneously in Kolonie-Deutsch and in English or standard German without losing the train(s) of thought or lapsing into the "wrong" language.

Comparisons of Amana's trilingualism with that of the Amish are perhaps inevitable. Like the Amish, speakers of Kolonie-Deutsch use their own dialect among themselves, and English for contacts outside the community. At that point, comparisons become less evident.[2] Unlike the Amish, whose acquaintance with written German is based primarily on familiarity with Scripture, hymnals, and devotional literature, most older Colonists were taught all subjects in *Schriftdeutsch,* speak it reasonably well on demand, and can often cite portions of secular German poems or folk songs from memory.

Stories abound of Amana residents traveling in Europe who found their German almost too good for comfort. A soldier from one of the villages was captured by the Germans during World War II and faced the dilemma of being able to understand his captors without daring to speak on his own behalf, lest he be taken for a German turncoat who had fought for the Americans. Other accounts circulate of tourists from Amana whose retention of a regional dialect is so striking that native Germans incorrectly assume that anyone who speaks the language so fluently will also understand local practices and etiquette. When such individuals fail to exercise the proper social graces, the faux pas is often received with far less tolerance than the blunder committed by a monolingual or imperfectly bilingual visitor.

Early in one of the interviews, a source who has traveled to Germany and whose work had brought her into contact with a number of native speakers of current German noted, "Ich probiere so viel wie möglich zu schwätzen wie ich daheim schwätze hier in Amana, aber wenn ich woanders bin wo die Leute sind von Deutschland, dann probiere ich besseres Deutsch zu schwätzen, ein bißl mehr Hochdeutsch." (I try, insofar as possible, to talk as I talk at home, here in Amana, but whenever I am somewhere else where there are German people from Germany, then I try to speak better German, a little bit more High German.)

"A little bit more High German" goes a long way, however! One speaker, though a strong supporter of teaching German in the local schools, made a special point of noting that the value of standard German lies in its usefulness for historical research or perhaps for conversing with visitors from Europe. For use in the Colonies, it is too *steif* 'stiff', and simply not always appropriate: "Das Schul-Deutsch ist gut, und ist recht, aber für unseren Zweck hier für die Kinder zu lernen hat es nicht [Sinn]." (School German is good, and it is correct, but for our purposes here, there is no sense in our children having to learn it.)

On one occasion when I visited a quilting session, the hostess assured a friend that she would have no trouble communicating with me. I had already spoken German and thereby demonstrated my potential ability to interact with the group. The fellow quilter who had heard my German glanced up furtively and snickered with benevolent amusement "der hat's gelernt" (he [merely] learned it, i.e., in school).

It was interesting to hear how a retired educator, whose classroom assignments included instruction in German, assessed the attitude in the seven villages toward persons who use "School German." During a formal interview held in German, she switched to English and asked me whether I would rather have her "talk in [the] Amana style." She then added in German: "Aber vielleicht ist es schwierig für mich, weil ich spreche eigentlich drei Sprachen, also Englisch, Hochdeutsch, und Kolonie-Deutsch, und alsmal alle drei zur selben Zeit." (But maybe it is difficult for me because actually I speak three languages, namely English, High German, and Amana German, and sometimes all three at the same time.) She then admitted that her Amana German "has become a little distorted because of the influence of High German, from studying and teaching it, which would of course have been in High German." She observed, "Ich muß . . . Achtung geben, da sonst hört sich [das] zu großartig an, wenn ich mit jemand von hier Hochdeutsch spreche . . . dann meinen sie, ja, was hat denn die vor?" (I need to pay attention, otherwise it sounds too pompous if I speak High German with someone from here . . . then they'll think, well, what does she think she's trying to do?)

One source, who frequently serves as a guide in the Museum of Amana History, commented that many visitors wanted to hear some German, but felt lost if it were not *familiar* German. Hence, he spent most of his days speaking English or, as occasion demanded, standard German. As a result, he wryly concluded, he could almost imitate Kolonie-Deutsch better than he could speak it!

If there is any difficulty communicating in current standard

German, it is for the generation of speakers now in early middle age through early retirement age who indeed learned to speak Kolonie-Deutsch at home but never acquired the formal rudiments of the language in school. A fairly typical comment came from a native of the Colonies whose family was stationed in Germany on military assignment. "They always understood me," she claimed, but the opposite was not always the case, and trying to eke out the most essential information often posed "a challenge" of considerable magnitude. Similarly, not all Amana speakers from this generation find it easy to follow the speech of the native German war brides who married Amana soldiers stationed in Europe. The language of these women is influenced by the schools of quite a different Germany than the one remembered by those forebears of today's Colonists who set up German-language programs in the seven villages.

This situation has led to a somewhat apologetic stance by some local speakers, who often unnecessarily excuse the German that is familiar to them as the product of humble circumstances: "You know, when we speak, wenn wir Deutsch sprechen zu Hause . . . wir tun nie von tiefen Subjekten sprechen . . . das ist grad' nicht getan bei uns." (You know, when we speak, when we speak German at home . . . we never speak about deep subjects . . . that just isn't done among us.) More than one speaker noted that s/he could speak easily if the partner in the conversation were an acquaintance, but scarcely otherwise. A typical comment might be this: "Weil ich weiß, daß ich nicht gelehrt bin, so ist mein Deutsch grad' nur Kolonie-Deutsch und nicht Deutsch-land-Deutsch . . . und so muß es gehen; wenn man gemütlich ist, kann man's ganz herrlich tun, aber wenn man wirklich probiert . . . dann geht's nicht." (Because I know that I'm not schooled, my German is just Kolonie-Deutsch and not Germany-German . . . and that is how it has to be; if one is relaxed, one can do it [i.e., speak German] wonderfully, but if one really tries . . . it just doesn't work.)

A small but important point is the fact that all speakers of Kolonie-Deutsch use the familiar pronoun of address, *du,* rather than the more formal *Sie,* "weil wir so bekannt mit einander [sind]" (because we are all so familiar with one another), and some local residents report involuntary negative feelings when the first signals are given that a more formal German is being spoken. Others feel it is more a matter of style than substance, claiming that the whole issue amounts to little more than the fact that speakers of Kolonie-Deutsch do not say "bitte schön, und sowas" (if you please, and such things).

As an aside, it might be noted that the use of the formal *Sie* was evidently more common in Amana in earlier years than it is today, though only in certain contexts. Church elders, for instance, might expect to be addressed, particularly by young persons, with the pronoun *Sie*.[3] The precedent for this antedates the period recalled by the oldest living residents of the Amana Colonies. In the extant correspondence with Christian Metz, we find that only Carl Ludwig Mayer, who was originally from a non-Inspirationist background, regularly addressed Metz with the pronoun *du;* all others used *Sie,* despite the fact that Metz himself frequently used *du* when writing to his coreligionists.[4] Whether the practice reflected respect for the individual or the office, it remains a small but salient indicator of the fact that social stratification was by no means absent in communal Amana.

While today some local residents exhibit reticence in the face of more prescriptively correct German, others—perhaps also prompted by a realization that their German is not School German—rise to the challenge of acquiring a more current standard German. One source, commenting on the use of German with his spouse in private, shared this observation: "Ich hab' auch gemerkt, seit wir in Deutschland zweimal auf Urlaub [waren], es ist nicht mehr so viel Kolonie-Deutsch wie es als war, wir probieren ein bißl besser, ein echtes Deutsch zu sprechen." (I've also noticed, since we were twice on vacation in Germany, that there isn't as much Kolonie-Deutsch as there used to be, we try to speak somewhat better, a genuine German.) When I asked just what an example of "genuine German" might be, the interview subject chose examples that specifically contrasted standard German and Kolonie-Deutsch. He and his wife now say *gesagt* instead of *gesacht* for the past participle of *sagen* 'to say', and increasingly refer to the German language as *Deutsch* rather than *Deitsch,* as is locally prevalent.

It is primarily vocabulary, however, that seems to catch the attention of most Colonists who become interested in differences between their German and that of the European fatherland. A local speaker observed that in current standard German "da sind Wörter wo [i.e., die] nicht dabei sind" (there are words that are just not present [in Kolonie-Deutsch]). He added that as soon as he found himself in a situation demanding the use of "more formal German," he sensed the need to grope for "the more proper method" of expressing himself. A fellow Colonist assessed the matter in rather categorical—though not altogether inaccurate—terms by claiming that speakers of Kolonie-Deutsch "don't know the [German] words for anything that was invented since 1842," the year in which members of the Community of True Inspiration set out for North America.

One result of this perceived leanness of current standard vocabulary is a sense among some speakers that European speakers of German can express things that the Colonist may feel but finds it difficult to put into words. The same individual who claimed that he and his fellow speakers of Kolonie-Deutsch didn't know the words for anything invented since 1842 noted that Germans, unlike individuals from Amana, might "say one thing and mean another." At first I misunderstood this comment, thinking he was lauding the integrity of his fellow Colonists and deploring the presumed duplicity of some Germans. When I asked just what this assertion was supposed to imply, my source explained that what he meant was that, in contrast to native Germans with whom he had spoken, he did not have command of vocabulary allowing expression of nuances going beyond an initial literal meaning of the words themselves.

One older Amana resident, having experienced no lack of contact with speakers of standard German, summarized it quite well. Using the locally prevalent *schwätzen* 'to speak', which carries the same meaning in parts of southwest Germany, but in more formal German means 'to prattle or gossip', she simply said "schwätzen ist one thing, aber verstehen, weißt du . . ." (speaking is one thing, but understanding, you know . . . [that is something else again]). From the overall context of the interview, it seemed clear that *verstehen* 'to understand' referred here not only to passive comprehension, but also to an understanding of how one might actively craft a correct statement in current German.

It is important to note that an increased awareness of the demands and conventions of standard German does not mean that a local speaker automatically develops lower esteem for Kolonie-Deutsch. One young adult speaker, who went to Germany with an enviable wordstock of grocery and household terms, found it linguistically and culturally challenging to deal with such activities as opening a bank account in a foreign country. Upon returning to Amana, she hoped to show off her newfound fluency in standard German but concluded after speaking with a grandmother and her friends that "it was the old ladies who spoke truly excellent German."[5]

Expressions of the awareness of language varieties extend beyond comparisons of Amana German and standard German. One local

speaker who has traveled widely in the United States and abroad chose
to comment on *schwätzen* 'to speak' by citing its synonyms used in
various regions of the German linguistic territory, such as High
German *sprechen* and Low German *schnacken,* familiar to some
speakers through firsthand contact with one or more of Iowa's Low
German–speaking communities, such as those in Butler and Grundy
counties.[6] Numerous speakers of Kolonie-Deutsch have had contact
with the Amish and are among the first to note that Amana German and
Pennsylvania (viz., Amish) German are quite different varieties of the
German language. A former teacher, who appears both fascinated and
horrified by the incorporation of so many English words into Amana
German, expressed the prevailing attitude among her fellow Colonists
that at least the German of her Amish friends seemed to have still more
English elements than does her beloved Kolonie-Deutsch!

No matter how mixed the feelings about the relative correctness of
their local German, Amana's residents remain unshaken in their loyalty
to the language. More than one speaker used terms such as *ingefleischt*
[i.e., *eingefleischt* literally: 'in the flesh'] to describe the deep-rooted
nature and function of Kolonie-Deutsch in their lives. A speaker with
personal and professional commitments that force him to use both
English and standard German extensively felt that his English and
(formal) German thought processes still involve conscious effort; for
Kolonie-Deutsch, these processes were unconscious and—as he noted
with evident pleasure—thoroughly natural. One widow even reported
dreaming that her late husband had appeared to tell her "Boy, es ist so
schön wo ich bin" (Boy, it is so beautiful where I am), and concluded
with evident relief "So denke ich als, im Himmel schwätzen sie auch
Deitsch" (So I sometimes think in heaven they speak German too)!
Since the verb expressing the heavenly speech act is *schwätzen* and the
kind of German spoken is *Deitsch,* one may fairly assume that it is
Kolonie-Deutsch, and not just any sort of German, that makes the life
to come "so schön."

Previous Scholarship

WHAT KOLONIE-DEUTSCH OFFERS the linguist is something at once very
old, yet very modern. Many forms of the local language are perceived
by visitors from the German-speaking regions of Europe as quaint or

even antiquated. At the same time, the language has incorporated numerous elements of American English and somewhat resembles a fossil come to life, complete with selective adaptations allowing it to function in an environment other than the one in which it first moved and had its being.

It is therefore not surprising that several major studies have been completed on Amana German. In 1935, only three years after the change from a system of theocratic communal governance to one with a division between the Amana Church Society for spiritual matters and the Amana Corporation for business affairs, Irving R. Johnson completed his doctoral dissertation on Amana German at the University of Iowa. Johnson's project was associated with the collection of recordings on aluminum disks that are not now readily accessible, and the findings presented in his dissertation have been superseded by subsequent scholarship. In 1941 Barbara J. Selzer, a native of Homestead, Iowa, completed an M.A. thesis at the University of Illinois on the speech of her home village. Included in this study is a rare example of a typical conversation in Kolonie-Deutsch from that period. Much of Selzer's work still merits serious consideration. Another scion of the Colonies, Lawrence L. Rettig, devoted his University of Iowa M.A. thesis (1967) and doctoral dissertation (1970) to the sounds and grammatical systems of Amana German. These graduate theses contain interesting samples of free discourse in Amana German. In 1969, Rettig published a study refuting earlier assertions of Carroll E. Reed and Herbert F. Wiese and in 1975 included a section on Amana German in his excellent history of the Amana Colonies since 1932, *Amana Today*. In 1977 Kurt Rein published the results of fieldwork carried out in the mid-1960s on vestiges of the Hessian dialect in a small circle of speakers living in Homestead, Iowa. In the early 1980s, while a Mellon Fellow in the University of Iowa's University House program, I began my own sociolinguistic fieldwork, which culminated in presentations to the Iowa Chapter of the American Association of Teachers of German (1984) and to the Linguistics Section of the Iowa Academy of Science (1984, and with Lanny Haldy and Barbara S. Hoehnle in 1989). In addition, several American scholars, including Jonathan Andelson in anthropology and James Dow in German and ethnography, and European colleagues, among others, Ulf-Michael Schneider in history and Frank Rehfeldt in linguistics, have carried out research that deserves to be more widely disseminated in this country.

The Present Study

MUCH OF THE BEST descriptive linguistic research has been carried out by persons whose roots are in the Amana Colonies (Barbara J. Selzer, Lawrence L. Rettig), and virtually all resultant publications have been directed at specialized academic audiences. Persons interested in the material of previous studies are encouraged to consult them. The goal of the present work is to address a somewhat broader readership of individuals with an interest in language variation and language use in the social context of the Amana Colonies.

The data presented here were gleaned from thirty-seven interviews involving fifty-four sources, conducted in 1989–1990 at the Amana Colonies.[7] Most of these interviews were carried out as part of a project sponsored by the Iowa Humanities Board/National Endowment for the Humanities to set up a tape archive of samples of Amana German at the Museum of Amana History; some half a dozen of these interviews are the outcome of efforts by collaborators in the tape archive project. In preparation for interview sessions, participants were asked to complete a questionnaire requesting personal background, information on frequency of language use with certain speaker-partners or for performing various language activity tasks, and opinions about language use and maintenance in the Colonies. The questionnaire and a summary of responses to selected questions are presented in the Appendix. While the present study does not focus on the analysis of quantifiable data, the reader is nevertheless encouraged to become familiar with the questionnaire at the outset, and to refer to it frequently.

All material is cited in the language chosen by the sources, with an English translation where appropriate. When it is primarily the narrative content of a statement (rather than linguistic form) that is essential to the point being made, standard German is used with the understanding that the typical Amana patterns of pronunciation and grammar noted by previous scholars are still operative, even if not always directly reflected by the material recorded here (which does, however, maintain original vocabulary and sentence structure). If a dialect or other nonstandard form enhances appreciation of a statement, it is intentionally maintained and rendered in orthography based on the conventions of modern standard German. This practice has historical and contemporary precedent in the Colonies themselves and in recent sociolinguistic studies such as those of Frank Rehfeldt and James R. Dow.

My guiding principle has been this: let the sources tell their own story. Invariably what they chose to say was more interesting than any points that I tried to elicit. The corpus of their contributions has suggested the final outline of this study far more effectively than had I chosen a rigidly imposed structure based on my own expectations. Put somewhat differently: the choice and relative importance given to the material presented here is intended to reflect the concerns and interests of the speaker-pool rather than the foci of my own private research agenda.

While few interview subjects hesitated to offer even the most sensitive information or opinions, many did ask to remain anonymous. In deference to this wish, I have tried to use only very general descriptions of the speakers whom I cite. My only regret is that, in not naming sources, I must forego the opportunity to openly thank many individuals whose special efforts assured the success of this project. My gratitude, though of necessity general in its expression, is deep and sincere: "Gerne sage ich Euch allen meinen recht innigen Dank!"

In a communal society, having to carry out even the most mundane tasks underlines the need for interdependence and cooperation, while providing an opportunity for social interaction. Although visible elements of lifestyle such as hair and clothing fashions changed over time, residents of the Amana Colonies maintained a deep appreciation for wholesome enjoyment of contact with familiar members of the community.

Peter Stuck

1928 A.A.A. CHAMPIONS

2

The Language Itself

What Would Our Parents Say?

IN HIS FIRST LETTER HOME, an Amana youth stationed with the U.S. military forces in Germany wrote to his mother to tell her that her German was outdated by a hundred years. Some months later the mother visited her son and recalls having learned that, indeed, "our [Amana] German is a hundred years behind." She lamented with evident chagrin that "wir haben nichts Neues seit unsere Eltern 'rüberkommen sind, und alles was neu war ist Englisches" (we don't have anything new [in the language] since our parents [i.e., ancestors] came over, and everything that was new is English). She concluded her account by repeating emphatically, "Our German *is* a hundred years behind."[1]

No doubt about it: Kolonie-Deutsch does preserve its share of old-fashioned elements. Some forms, such as the demonstratives *derselbige* (now more commonly *derselbe*) 'the same one' or *etwelche* (now more commonly *etliche* or *einige*) 'certain ones', are not even found in many popular dictionaries of the German language and are classified as archaic in more comprehensive lexical works. Still other words and phrases have passed out of daily use for the majority of European speakers of German but survive intact in the language of specific regions or social strata. Examples of such items appear at points throughout this chapter.

Strictly speaking, it would not have been necessary for the serviceman's mother to take the trip to Germany in order to learn about the old-fashioned character of her community's speech. Amana residents, particularly those who regularly meet the public, have long

since learned to offer patient and vaguely bemused smiles to visitors
from Europe (and even from parts of North America) who take delight
in regaling Colonists with this observation: folks in the seven villages
speak German just the way that the visitors' parents or grandparents
did. The person charmed by Amana German's supposed quaintness
may, however, fail to consider all pertinent factors. True, the visitor's
grandmother or grandfather may have spoken a regional variety of
German and may have made heavy use of colloquial forms. They may
indeed have been unable to do otherwise. When one suddenly encounters in Amana the thoroughly unabashed use of once-familiar forms that
elsewhere have given way to School German, it is only too easy to
conclude that one has chanced upon a rare remnant from the past, a
sort of linguistic fossil as it were. At times this is true. At other times
additional considerations need to be taken into account.

Let us look at a few examples shared by Amana residents of what
they believe to be—or have been told are—evidence for the antiquated
nature of their speech.

Few bits of information are more important to travelers than the
location of restroom facilities. It is then perhaps not surprising that
almost every Amana native who has been abroad has a bathroom story
to tell. The term in the seven villages for 'toilet' is *Abtritt* [literally:
'departure, leave', as in 'to make one's departure' or 'to take one's
leave'], a somewhat antiquated slang term for that most vital of all
public and private accommodations. When a Colonist goes abroad and
expresses a need for the *Abtritt,* s/he is often met with looks of
amazement and not infrequently with a comment to the effect that such
terms are just not used anymore. Many of those who report episodes
of this kind (and there exists no lack of such raconteurs) interpret the
surprised reaction of native Germans as evidence of Amana German's
old-fashioned character. Another possibility is that the colloquial nature
of the term, as much as any quaintness as such, could have provoked
the reaction that nowadays one would assume that folks simply don't
say such things in unfamiliar circles!

A number of common Kolonie-Deutsch vocabulary items are
historically associated with a particular regional dialect (e.g., *gelbe
Rüben* instead of *Karotten* as the term for 'carrots'). Hence, a speaker
from Amana who visits Germany may very well find that not all
Germans use or readily respond to the linguistic conventions received
in former years from old-time Colonists. This may lead to the
conclusion that the language of the speaker's linguistic forebears has

since passed from the scene, except perhaps in such seemingly out-of-the-way places as the Amana Colonies. If the same speaker were to visit a particular part of the German linguistic territory, however, s/he might find—as is often recounted by those who have done so—that the Germans of the region are delighted to meet a visitor from America who is able to converse in a strikingly genuine version of the local speech patterns.

An example of a regional form that has become the norm in Kolonie-Deutsch is the word *als*. Throughout most of the German-speaking territory, *als* serves as a conjunction, either to introduce a subordinate clause whose verb is in the past tense or in certain expressions involving the comparative degree of adjectives and adverbs. An etymologically distinct, yet homonymic, form *als* (or *alsmal*) exists in Upper Alemanic (extreme southwestern German and Swiss) dialects and in the speech of the Amana Colonies. Kolonie-Deutsch *als[mal]* differs significantly from standard German *als*: it serves as an adverb rather than as a conjunction and conveys the meaning 'sometimes' or occasionally 'once upon a time', as in "ich tue es auch als" (I also do it sometimes), "ich weiß nicht, ob ich als mehr Englisch oder Deutsch schwätze" (I don't know whether I sometimes speak more English or German), or "was ich verstehe und was ich alsmal nicht verstehe" (what I understand and what I sometimes do not understand). To make matters even more complicated, Kolonie-Deutsch often uses alternative forms, illustrated elsewhere in this study, where one might expect to find standard German *als*. One can easily enough imagine the reaction of a speaker of Amana German who learns that s/he has been using high-frequency vocabulary with the "wrong" meaning, and even as the "wrong" part of speech, at least as far as School German is concerned. The fact that these and other nonstandard forms common in Kolonie-Deutsch may represent the survival of usage patterns once common enough in another era or area offers little consolation to confused speakers.

Still other extralinguistic factors may play a role. One example of language use that shows differing cultural values in the European homeland and in the Amana Colonies is the mealtime blessing:

> Komm Herr Jesus
> Sei unser Gast
> Und segne,
> Was Du uns bescheret hast.

(Come Lord Jesus
Be our guest
And may these gifts
From Thee be blest.)

In a conversation with a European visitor, one Colonist was told that "only the farmers" still recite this prayer. The Amana resident who recounted this episode proudly recited these lines as an example of gloriously old-fashioned German. The truth is that nonagriculturalists in Germany and elsewhere in Europe and North America still love and recite this simple text. What the visitor may have wanted to convey was the idea that in a European society, which is rapidly losing its assumptions about the importance of the church, one would only find such spontaneous expressions of piety among simpler folk who had not yet been fully caught up in the fast-paced whirl of secularized urban life. For some, what may seem as old-fashioned as the language itself is its function in transmitting values once prevalent in continental German society, but now considered by many to be obsolescent.

But Is It German?

LAWRENCE RETTIG, in his 1970 doctoral dissertation, has done an excellent job of presenting the typical grammatical paradigms of Amana German. No attempt is made here to offer still another systematic grammatical study. What needs to be presented in this study, however, is a sampling of characteristic forms of Kolonie-Deutsch. Like all products of human behavior and interaction, they have explicable, even if not always immediately evident, origins. Stated somewhat differently: even the so-called "nonstandard" forms of Kolonie-Deutsch usually prove, upon closer inspection, to be vestiges of the influence of a particular variety of German. These language forms have a recognizable past, or they are the outcome of known linguistic processes of change, whose operation may be expected over time in any living language. In other words, under conducive social conditions Kolonie-Deutsch would have the potential for future development.

Some features are so common in colloquial spoken German that one needs to be reminded that they are also part of the characteristic patterns of Amana German. An example of this is the loss of the final conjugational and declensional [n], as in *komme* for *kommen, Fraue* for *Frauen*. Other features are less widespread among nonlocal speakers of German and deserve separate mention here.

A person trained in School German often cringes to hear *mir* 'we' and considerably less frequently *dir* 'you (plural subject)' in place of *wir* and *ihr*. These Kolonie-Deutsch pronouns are well-attested colloquial forms throughout broad reaches of the German linguistic territory and may well puzzle the prescriptive grammarian, since they are homonymic with standard German *mir* (indirect object) 'me' and *dir* (familiar singular indirect object) 'you'. The origin of these seeming anomalies, unkindly labeled by some as Me-Tarzan-You-Jane German, however, has been widely recognized by linguists for decades. Certain sentence patterns require the subject pronoun (*wir, ihr*) to occur after its verb; in these positions, the operation of various phonological processes produced the forms *mir* 'we' and *dir* 'you (plural subject)', especially in the southern regions of the German-speaking territory. The resultant pronouns eventually found acceptance in sentence patterns other than those that originally fostered their use.

Another pronoun form familiar in many local German dialects is *wo* [standard German: 'where'] as the subject, less frequently as the direct object form, of the relative pronoun: "der Mann, wo [standard German: *der*] gestern hier war" (the man who was here yesterday). The extended use of *wo* is carried still one step further both here and in parts of Germany by its use in place of standard German *als,* as previously mentioned, to introduce a subordinate clause in the past tense, for example, "wo [standard German: *als*] wir Kits [i.e., Kinder] waren" (when we were children). During my student days in southwest Germany, I encountered a young woman who complained that an older mutual acquaintance knew only one way to connect relative and subordinate clauses to the main sentence, and that was with the word *wo*. Although she exaggerated somewhat, there was more than a germ of truth in her statement. Hence, Kolonie-Deutsch sentences such as those just cited cause me, as a trained grammarian, to make a mental note of correction; yet the Kolonie-Deutsch forms themselves are unquestionably more genuinely German than the attempts of many learners who misapply the rules of grammar and produce something totally unfamiliar to any native speaker.

Another pattern worth noting, and one well documented in the historical annals of the German language, is the use of the dative case, primarily to signal the indirect object and the concepts 'to' and 'for', as a substitute for the genitive case whose main function is to indicate possession. One encounters sentences such as "meinem Vater seine Seite" [standard German: "die Seite meines Vaters"; more commonly, väterlicherseits] (my father's side [of the family]) or "(dem) Brad seine Oma" [standard German: "Brads Oma"] (Brad's grandmother).

Some of the characteristic patterns of Kolonie-Deutsch may appear at first to be direct translations from English. One might, for instance, literally translate the form of *tun* 'to do' in the Kolonie-Deutsch sentence "wann tust du eben Deutsch usen?" (just when do you use German?) and come up with good idiomatic English. Word-for-word equivalence does not, however, necessarily mean borrowing from English. Although reminiscent of English, the use of *tun* 'to do' as an auxiliary verb is familiar enough in southern German dialects. In the clause "jetzt wenn du eben sterben tust" (now when you die), there is no exact English equivalent of the auxiliary verb and little likelihood that the form results from English influence on the speaker's German. Variation from the norm, rather than suggesting something less than genuine German, may be the very factor that attests to the historical authenticity of many forms of Kolonie-Deutsch.

What all this means is that, rather than being called *Deutschverderber* 'spoilers of German' as some in fact label themselves, speakers of Kolonie-Deutsch ought to be regarded as preservers of particular features inherited from a very colloquial and/or regional variety of the German language.

Where Are the Limits?

ALL THIS DOES NOT MEAN that one can explain away every unusual form as a carryover from the linguistic patrimony of earlier Colonists. At times the speaker of Kolonie-Deutsch appears to be truly uncertain what form to use and, as an expedient, creates a hybrid. Such instances may provide evidence that the language is experiencing those normal processes of change that attest to its continuing vitality or, quite the opposite, that its speakers are not fully in control of an uncertain and obsolescent medium of communication. It is not always easy to tell the difference.

As a rule, the comparative form of a German adjective or adverb is followed by *als,* as in *mehr als* 'more than'. In Amana, however, it is far from uncommon to hear *mehr wie* or *mehr denn* / *mehr dann*. There are, in fact, cases in standard German where the positive degree is used with *wie* to express comparison, for example *so gut wie* 'as good as'. Here the speaker of Kolonie-Deutsch frequently uses *als* rather than the expected *wie*: "Ich würde die Geographie nicht so gut kennen als ich tue" (I wouldn't know geography as well as I do). In other words, *als* and *wie* can cross the lines of generally accepted usage patterns with each appearing where the pupil of formal German might expect the other. To be extra sure that all bases are covered, and perhaps not being altogether certain just which bases need to be covered, some speakers will produce hypercorrect—or, as it were, hyper*incorrect*—phrases with both *als* and *wie,* for example, *niedriger als wie das* 'lower than that'.

No grammatical category in Kolonie-Deutsch hovers more precariously over the line separating variation on and aberration from the linguistic norm than do the verbs.

As in many German-American communities, one encounters semantic extensions that appear to reflect the influence of English. A well-attested illustration from numerous German-speaking communities in the American diaspora is the verb *gleichen* 'to appear'. It is used with the meaning 'to like', a semantic borrowing due to such combined forces as similarity of sounds, the possible translation of *gleichen* as 'to be (a)like', and the fact that the German adjective *gleich* can convey the meaning 'like (i.e., alike, similar)'. Therefore, in Amana one can say "ich gleich sie alle gut" (I like them all [equally] well) or, as in English with a complementary infinitive, "ich gleich zu reimen in Deutsch" (I like to rhyme in German).

In Kolonie-Deutsch, the verb *gucken* 'to (take a) look', like English *to look,* often carries the meaning 'to appear; to resemble'. Standard German would require *aussehen, ausschauen,* perhaps even *ausgucken,* or *ähneln*. One hears statements such as "das guckt mir auch gerade so" (that is just how it looks/appears to me, too) or "er guckt wie sein Vater" (he looks like/resembles his father). Intransitive *anfangen* 'to begin' is used transitively, as in, "ich fange das an" [standard German: "ich beginne das / ich fange damit an"] 'I begin that'. Occasionally one hears *lernen* 'to learn' used in a manner reminiscent of some colloquial varieties of English, with the meaning 'to teach'. Whether this latter example necessarily reflects any English influence is open to discussion since southern German colloquial speech does have forms such as "er lernt mir Deutsch" for standard "er lehrt mich Deutsch" (he teaches me German).

Certain German verbs predictably change the stem vowel in the second- and third-person singular forms. In Amana the vowel change often fails to take place, resulting in forms such as

fallen 'to fall', *du fallst* 'you fall' (instead of *du fällst*);
lesen 'to read', *er lest* 'he reads' (instead of *er liest*);
sehen 'to see', *du sehst* 'you see' (instead of *du siehst*).[2]

While it is true that in certain southern German dialects the vowel mutation often does not take place, and the forms cited here are far from incomprehensible, their use in Amana is frequently inconsistent for a given speaker; overall speech pattern may not be predictably characteristic in other respects of the German dialect territory where such lack of vowel mutation is most common. In other words, the appearance of these forms in Kolonie-Deutsch may plausibly represent the widespread use of readily available—albeit perhaps originally regional—features to simplify the seeming complexities of the verbal system, rather than strict preservation of local speech patterns brought to Amana by earlier speakers from the German homeland.

Another category of interest that clearly merits a separate study is the past participle. Several forms with long histories and continued regional usage in the German language remain in Kolonie-Deutsch, such as *kommen* and *gangen* without the otherwise near-ubiquitous participial prefix *ge-*: "bist [du] kommen [rather than *gekommen*]?" (did you come?) or "in die Schule gangen [rather than *gegangen*] hat" (had gone to school). It is ironic that in the second example, with its traditionally conservative past participle, the expected auxiliary *sein* 'to be', which is used with certain intransitive verbs to form the perfect tense, has given way to an English-influenced form of *haben* 'to have' (*gangen hat* rather than *[ge]gangen ist*). Within a single clause, we find the vestiges of an earlier stage in the developmental history of the German language alongside evidence from the English-speaking world in which the Amana Colonies are situated today.

Possibly historical remnants, yet also conceivably the result of the reduction of irregularities in the verbal system over time, are past participles such as *gewißt* [standard German *gewußt,* though much earlier *gewißt* is attested] 'known', *gedenkt* [alongside standard German *gedacht*] 'thought', and *ausgerennt* [standard German *ausgerannt*] 'run out'. All of these Kolonie-Deutsch forms are derived from verbs whose standard past participles combine regular and irregular elements. The suffix is generally characteristic of regular verbs but with a vowel mutation reminiscent of stem-change verbs. Though forms such as *gewißt* and *gedenkt* occur only sporadically in German-speaking Europe, they have become the norm in the Amana Colonies.

A tendency toward regularity within the system does not, however, necessarily mean wholesale elimination of all complexity. One typically German construction, frequently felt by nonnative speakers of the language to be fraught with complication, is the use of multiple infinitives in forming the perfect tenses of certain verbs (most frequently the modal auxiliaries) whose complement is still another verb in the infinitive. These constructions are used heavily in Amana German, and one could cite countless examples from local speech. One speaker correctly used the multiple-infinitive construction to describe the end of the communal era: "es hätte nicht so einerlei [einfach] fortgehen können" (it could not have gone on so simply). Nonstandard variations of word order are not uncommon, however, such as the transposed sequence of infinitives, "ich habe so Achtung wollen geben" (I wanted so [much] to pay attention), or a change in the position of the auxiliary verb, "[der,] wo dich sehen hat wollen" ([the person] who wanted to see you). In the use of multiple infinitives, simplification through regularization and reduction in the number of possible patterns have not yet taken place.

Well-attested yet not altogether fully consistent in local speech are multiple-infinitive constructions with still other verbs used in a modal capacity, for example, with *brauchen*: "wir haben gar nicht viel Englisch sprechen brauchen" (we didn't need to speak much English at all). We even find the compound *kennenlernen* 'to get to know, become acquainted with' appearing in multiple-infinitive constructions, though such usage is eschewed by prescriptive grammarians who point out that *kennen* is a prefix to, rather than a complement of, *lernen*. This fine point of distinction is evidently not appreciated by all speakers of Kolonie-Deutsch, and hence from one and the same source I was able to document the standard German past participle *kennengelernt* and a multiple-infinitive construction, "so habe ich ihn kennen lernen" (thus I got to know him).

In addition to these grammatical notabilia, there are also changes in vocabulary reflecting active semantic evolution within the language. This has been a feature of considerable interest to linguists for some time. Barbara Selzer, in her 1941 M.A. thesis, gives a list of Kolonie-Deutsch lexical items not found in standard German or that have acquired a new semantic valence in the speech of the seven villages.[3]

Many of these neologisms reflect the pervasive influence of English, as will be discussed. What should not be overlooked is that apart from any influx of English elements, Kolonie-Deutsch displays exactly the same patterns of coinage and change that characterize any living language.

Familiar to speakers of English is the use of an originally negative term as an hyperbolic intensifier: I am terribly (awfully, frightfully, horribly) sorry. A similar phenomenon occurs in Kolonie-Deutsch. In the Amana Colonies, someone who does something very well does it "saumäßig gut" (sow-like well). Recalling her youth, one local resident talked about when she was "gräßlich jung" (horribly young), and another recounted her experiences with a stern teacher for whom everyone had "ganz jämmerlich Respekt" (altogether wretched [much] respect).

There are a number of terms that appear to have been coined in the Colonies. Not having been familiar with the camera in Germany [standard German uses *der Fotoapparat* or *die Kamera*], the earlier residents of the seven villages needed to come up with some term for this new item in their lives. Rather than adopt the English word, the Colonists coined the term *der Abnehmkasten* 'the take-down [i.e., recording] box' for this product of American culture. Despite early injunctions against photography and the display of pictures in the home, the camera gained increasing popularity, and a rich variety of early photographs by both Colonists and outsiders is represented in the collections of the Museum of Amana History.[4] Another compound of familiar German elements is *die Dreckschipp(e)* 'the filth scoop' for 'dustpan'. It is interesting that the standard German terms *die Müllschaufel* 'the refuse shovel' and *die Kehrschaufel* 'the sweeping shovel' convey much the same literal meaning. A word unfamiliar to most speakers of standard German is *die Gauntschel,* the local term for the lawn swing with facing benches that has become such a familiar feature in and around the seven villages. For all practical purposes, this term is Kolonie-Deutsch, rather than standard German, vocabulary.

Evidently rhubarb first became familiar in America, where the Colonists combined English *pie* and German *der Stengel* 'the stalk, stem' and dubbed the plant *Peistengel.* One source commented, "Ich denke, das haben sie gerade translated, die Stengel vor zum pie machen, ja, wir sagen alle Peistengel zu rhubarb, Rhubarber [Rhabarber] ist das deutsche Wort." (I think they just translated that [term meaning] the stalks for making pie, yes, we all say *Peistengel* for rhubarb, *Rhubarber* [actually, *Rhabarber*] is the German word.) A perceptive local speaker compared *Peistengel* to the American English dialect term *pieplant*. Whether there is a connection beyond coincidence or whether this is in fact a loan translation with hybrid English and German elements remains to be investigated. What is certain is that the term *Peistengel* is so thoroughly established in the local vocabulary that the English element, *pie,* is no longer felt to be intrusive. Pie, however, is not a familiar feature of German cuisine, and hence has no exact alternate designation in the German language. If anything, it is the standard German term for rhubarb that strikes local speakers as being somehow foreign or unfamiliar.

Something Old, Something New, Something Borrowed . . .

WHAT THE EXAMPLES JUST CITED demonstrate is Amana German's resilience, adaptability, and potential for growth and change. If Kolonie-Deutsch is indeed caught in the throes of obsolescence, that fact is first of all due to changing social forces, and only secondarily to any loss of vitality in the language itself. Hence, in looking at evidence for the influence of English on the German of the Amana Colonies, we find ourselves confronted by the result, rather than by the cause, of changing patterns of language use.

Many of the speakers cited in this study completed a questionnaire that asked the survey participants, among other things, to indicate with a check mark which language was preferred for certain activities. One of the first individuals to return a questionnaire had intentionally placed all of the check marks in such a way that both German and English were marked as the language of preference. Perhaps, as suggested by one person close to the research effort, neither was the clearly preferred language. At any rate the overlapping check marks offer a telling representation of the situation in the Amana Colonies, where, as has been noted with a bit of tongue-in-cheek wryness, it is possible to be simultaneously bilingual in both languages.

An older source displayed obvious relish in recounting tales passed to him by his grandmother of the earliest confrontation by his linguistic forebears with the English language. The Inspirationists originally settled at Ebenezer, New York, and three days after their arrival (or so the story goes), English started creeping into the language of the recent immigrants. What stands as a fact is the presence, even in early records, of such loanwords as *die Fence* (or *die Fens*).[5] This should not be too surprising: too little attention has been drawn to the fact that a number of Inspirationists prepared for migration to America by making special efforts to study the English language prior to departure for the new homeland.[6]

By 1932 when the communal theocratic system gave way to a division between church and day-to-day administrative functions, enough English had made its way into the language of the Colonies that the event came to be known as *der Change*. Today one refers to this as the period "wo mir 'rübergechanged sind" (when we changed over). Within a decade of the Change, Barbara Selzer was able to offer a long list of English loanwords, organized by semantic category, that were current in the Colonies.[7] It is doubtful that all of these terms made their way into Kolonie-Deutsch only, or even primarily, after 1932.

Before I had become a familiar presence in the Colonies, a local resident took pity on me and assured me that I need not worry if I found myself unable to grasp everything that was said in Kolonie-Deutsch: "[Even if] you cannot understand any of our German . . . if you listen very carefully to two people talking, you can pick out the key words because they are always in English." While I cannot agree altogether with this assertion, it carries more than just a bit of truth and also helps me to place into more critical perspective statements that children no longer learn fluent German because they have "picked up . . . English from the television," or from some other external source. The truth of the matter is that the children need not go as far as the television set to hear plenty of English.

Even at an earlier period, many of the emotionally laden interjections of Kolonie-Deutsch were English, and so it is not surprising that today one can hardly carry on a conversation in German in one of the seven villages without hearing "you bet," "well all right," "by gosh," and similar exclamations.[8] In a sense the Kolonie-Deutsch conversation is one spoken in German, but punctuated in English.

Among the most heavily borrowed categories of words are nouns. There is certainly nothing surprising about the fact that terms ranging from *homebrew* to *Medicare* and from *light bulbs* to *bums* have made their way into Kolonie-Deutsch. At a quilting session two participants were discussing whether the particular type of thread being used should be called *der Zwirn* 'thread, yarn' or *der Faden* 'thread, cord'. An eminently practical solution—that enjoyed spontaneous and universal acceptance—was a proposal to call the item by its familiar American brand name.

Still other common English nouns such as *fun* and *turn* have
entered the local German language; this occurs with greater frequency
in those instances where the English noun may appear as a predicate
noun after the verb *to be* (*to be fun, to be one's turn,* etc.), whereas the
German equivalent, in contrast, typically requires an idiomatic
construction involving another verb (*Spaß machen,* [literally: 'to make
fun'], *an der Reihe sein* [literally: 'to be at the turn']). In Kolonie-
Deutsch, one might hear "das ist ja fun" (that surely is fun) or "jetzt
ist es mein turn" (now it's my turn); one might also hear standard
German "das macht ja Spaß" or "ich bin jetzt an der Reihe" to express
the same ideas.

This touches upon a general principle observed in Kolonie-Deutsch
and common in any number of situations involving contact between the
language of an ethnic minority and the language of the dominant
culture: when a word is borrowed from American English, it often
brings with it the idiomatic construction of the source language. In the
case of nouns, the phenomenon can be traced back to the earliest days
of the Amana Colonies. Although we have no extant letter of Christian
Metz in the English language, his German letters contain a fair number
of English terms, particularly nouns.[9] In those letters we find expressions such as "auf der Rail Road fahren" (to ride on the railroad
[standard German: "mit dem Zug/mit der Bahn fahren" to ride with the
train]).[10] An investigation into the historical and contemporary loan
syntax of borrowed idiomatic expressions in Amana German offers the
prospect of abundant and interesting results.

Even when recognizable German nouns are used, the influence of
English may be abundantly evident. This is especially common when
German and English words share a common origin and may have
partially overlapping semantic ranges. Hence German *der Weg* 'way,
road' is often used to translate English *way,* even if the meaning is
'way, manner', for which standard German requires a different word
altogether: "[A certain third party] hat's diesen Weg erklärt" (explained
it this way). Only rarely will a speaker correct such English-influenced
semantic borrowings. One source wished to clarify a procedure and
interjected, "No, der andere Weg, [and then, in standard German]
nein, anders[r]um" (No, [do it] the other way, no, the other way
around). For the most part, however, it never occurs to the speaker of
Kolonie-Deutsch to make such corrections: the term in question has
undergone a thorough process of linguistic naturalization and no longer

strikes the speaker as foreign or intrusive.

Other common examples of such overly facile translations abound. Colony residents send their children to *die Hochschul(e)* 'high school', a semantic shift reflecting American cultural realities: in Germany the term designates a university-level institution. The Amana farmer is as often as not *der Farmer,* rather than *der Bauer* [standard German: 'the farmer']; *der Bauer* is now for some Kolonie-Deutsch speakers 'the builder, construction tradesman' (from *bauen* 'to build').

Speakers of Kolonie-Deutsch seeking a deeper understanding of all this might look for *die Meinung* 'meaning' [standard German: 'opinion'; rigid arbiters of the language would insist on *die Bedeutung* 'the significance']. This use of *die Meinung* is no doubt due to its phonetic similarity to English *meaning,* as well as to the partially overlapping—though semantically distinct—English translation of meaning in German of *meinen* 'to believe, intend, mean' and *bedeuten* 'to mean, signify'.

There are also numerous blends of German and English lexical elements. A noteworthy example on several points is the compound *der Küchenbaß* 'the kitchen boss' (in the communal era, the woman in charge of one of the large kitchens serving several families). In addition to the phonological naturalization of the originally foreign element *boss,* the fact that there exists no other more "purely German" term for this office witnesses to the fact that such hybrid compounds were a well-established, and indeed well-accepted, fact of life prior to the Change of 1932!

I tried to determine whether there was any evidence that the term *Küchenbaß* might contain as one of its constituent elements the German word *der Baas* 'the boss'. All those whom I queried assured me that the origin was English *boss,* even though *der Baas* does appear in earlier German texts composed in the Amana Colonies, including several humorous vignettes cited in Chapter 3. In other words, the perception—whether historically accurate or not—is that this term, linked as it is with the unique tradition of the Amana Colonies, might be viewed as simply another example of the long-standing and pervasive infiltration of English into the local German idiom.[11]

If the underlying concept of a compound noun is itself borrowed from English, there is a fairly good chance that only those elements with recognizable cognates in both languages will be Germanized. A typical example is the hybrid compound *Pocketbuch* 'purse', borrowed from English *pocketbook*. German has no commonly derived cognate of *pocket;* thus, the English term is taken over without even the faintest hint of phonological compromise. *Book* and *Buch,* by contrast, are easily recognized as words of shared origin and hence the second element of the compound is German. Although at times the contrary might be cited, the governing principle seems to be this: if the English form is distinct in its difference, accept it on its own terms; if it strikes a note of familiarity, strive to accentuate the elements of similarity.[12]

Verbs, alongside nouns, are the grammatical category most influenced by English. This process manifests itself in several ways.

Those who are familiar with both languages instantly recognize the literal, albeit nonidiomatic, loan translation of English in such terms as *ufgucken* 'to look up' (e.g., in a dictionary) [standard German: *nachschlagen* or even more colloquial *nachgucken*]. A verb particularly subject to such word-for-word translation, as in the semantic borrowing from English leading to entire loan phrases, is *nehmen* 'to take': "wir haben ihn zum Essen genommen" (we took him to eat) [standard German: *eingeladen,* or perhaps *mitgenommen*], "sie hat Deutsch genommen" (she took German [in school]) [standard German: *gelernt*], "das hat nicht lang genommen" (that didn't take long) [standard German: *gedauert*]. Even compounds of *nehmen* appear in such translations: "wir können auch ein bißl Zeit ausnehmen" (we can take a little time out) [standard German: "wir können auch eine Pause einlegen" or "wir können uns ein bißchen Zeit nehmen"].

Most of the English impact on Kolonie-Deutsch verbs is even more apparent than these literal translations, and the next level of influence is that of German verbs taking on the specific meaning of a phonologically similar, though semantically distinct, English cognate. We hear, for instance, via the process of semantic borrowing, that a certain person "hat viel Zeit gespendet" (spent a lot of time) at a certain undertaking [standard German demands *verbringen* 'to pass or spend time' rather than *spenden* 'to donate']. Due recognition is given to "jemand, [der] was zu opfern hat" (someone who has something to offer) [standard German: *an[zu]bieten* 'to offer, i.e., contribute']. When I expressed some uncertainty about an issue of common interest, my conversation partner responded, "Das wundre ich gerade" (I'm [also] wondering that just now) [standard German: "das frage ich mich gerade"].

Confusion of *meinen* 'to mean, be of the opinion' and *bedeuten* 'to mean, signify' are quite common (see the previous discussion of *Meinung* and *Bedeutung*). One speaker who now converses mostly in

English still finds a special spot in the heart for German and confided, "Zu mir meint das Deutsche viel mehr" (To me the German means much more) [standard German: "mir bedeutet das Deutsche viel mehr"]. Ironically, the German language that means so much to the speaker is used in this instance in a patently English mode of expression. Another Amana resident may have attempted to avoid this pitfall through use of *bedeuten* in sharing the view that "[Gott] hat uns bedeutet . . . [seine Knechte] zu sein" (God meant us to be his servants) [standard German: "Gott hat uns dazu bestimmt, seine Knechte zu sein"]. In these and countless other instances, the best way to understand Kolonie-Deutsch is to ask what English vocabulary and idiom might lie behind a given statement.

The most direct and, indeed, blatant influence, however, consists of an English verb being taken over with little or no phonological adaptation into Kolonie-Deutsch speech. As one source put it: "Es ist so der Gebrauch hier, daß man ein englisches verb [pronounced in this instance as English *verb* rather than as German *Verb*] nimmt und macht eine deutsche Endung . . . oder vielleicht gar keine Endung, gerade nur so ein kleiner [sic] slur." (It is the custom here to take an English verb and add a German ending . . . or maybe no ending at all, just a little slur.) Another local resident provided a written list of just such hybrid derivations, which often contain the trappings of both the English and German grammatical systems.

"Kein attention ge*paid*" (Paid no attention)
"Hast du dein test ge*passed*?" (Did you pass your test?)
"Er ist 'naus ge*kicked* worden." (He was kicked out.)
"Kannst du das aus*straighten*en?" (Can you straighten that out?)
"Kannst du mich uf*pick*en?" (Can you pick me up?)
"Ich *pick* dich 'uf'." (I'll pick you up.)

To this list one might add any number of examples, including *braggen* 'to brag', *explainen* 'to explain', *fixen* 'to fix', *teachen* 'to teach', and *usen* 'to use', all of which are quite common in Kolonie-Deutsch, despite the fact that they replace German verbs whose use poses no idiomatic or other special linguistic considerations that would prompt a speaker to favor a borrowed term.

As a curious sidelight, one source seemed able to describe acts of crime only with English verbs to which German affixes had been added. No one from local circles seemed surprised to hear about this speaker's choice of vocabulary in referring to the unfortunate victims who had been *gerobbed* 'robbed' and *gemurdered* 'murdered' in a wave of violence in a nearby city. No doubt, news of these crimes had been picked up from the English-language media, and specific key terms from the source fixed themselves in English in the mind of the speaker.

Only occasionally is the English pronunciation modified. When the verbs *sneak* and *smoke* are used in Kolonie-Deutsch, the initial sound is similar to that of English *shoe*. The more common pattern, however, is to adopt the loanword without further adaptation beyond the addition of a prefix and/or suffix: "was du explainst" (what you explain); "ich habe auch ein bißl geworried" (I also worried a bit); or without even that much accommodation to the norms of the German language, "ich habe sie clipped" (I clipped them), or "frisch admitted" (freshly admitted [to the hospital]). The only pattern that I discerned in the use or nonuse of grammatical affixes was that past participles of English verbs originally ending in [t] typically do not add a suffix, despite the fact that a suffix would be the norm in both languages: "das hat gecount" (that counted), "gut getreat" (well treated). Evidently an unflinchingly strict application of this principle accounts for "[hat] gemeet" ([has] met), where the specific demands of the English verbal system—in this instance, change of the vowel in the past participle—yield to the prevailing patterns of Kolonie-Deutsch.

The fact that one can easily identify the English origin of these verbs does not mean that they are necessarily less likely to enjoy full integration into the language. This point is illustrated by the many verbs that are combined with the so-called separable prefixes, common to anyone familiar with the German language in a more than casual way, to form hybrid derivatives. We then find 1932 cited as the year in which the villages were *übergechanged, 'nübergechanged,* or *'rübergechanged* 'changed over' to a new system of governance; children are *abgedropped* 'dropped off' and *ufgepicked* 'picked up' at a day-care center; several local businesses were *mitinvolved* 'co-involved' in a venture; one family found itself *umgemoved* 'moved around' quite a bit from one residence to another over the years.

Verbal syntax, even where purely German verbs are involved, may also belie an underlying English bias. A common example of this borrowed syntax is the English use of a relative pronoun or adverb and an infinitive phrase, a construction that must be rendered by a relative or subordinate clause in standard German. Hence two older Colonists talked about what they had learned in earlier years: one had learned "wie zu schreiben" (how to write) and another "wie zu Besen machen" (how to make brooms). The statement from another conversation seemed to apply here, that a knowledgeable person "hat [ihnen] gezeigt was zu machen" (showed them what to do). Had one wished to express these ideas in standard German, it would have been necessary to use separate clauses to explain that the individuals in question had learned how one writes, how one makes brooms, and what one must do ("wie man schreibt, wie man Besen macht, was man machen muß").

Still other parts of speech show the unmistakable impact of English. One constantly encounters the use of adjectives such as *handy, original, plenty,* and *sure,* especially as predicate adjectives, where German requires no added ending: "das ist handy" (that is handy). Adverbs and adverbial phrases include *anyhow, in fact, at least, offhand, really, recently, somehow,* and even *upstairs* and *downstairs.* Prepositions are rarely borrowed, except perhaps where an often-used English phrase comes to mind, as in "after dem Change" (after the [1932] Change). On the other hand, examples abound of prepositional complements to verbs that are literal translations of English.

English	Kolonie-Deutsch	standard German
search for	suchen für	suchen nach
driven by (motors)	getrieben bei	getrieben von
come from (originate)	kommen von	kommen aus

One often hears *vor* 'before' used, as it sometimes was earlier in the history of the language, where one might expect *für* 'for'. Whether we are dealing with the influence of near-homonymic English *for* or a vestige of older usage patterns is not always altogether clear.

Conjunctions, like prepositions, are seldom taken over intact, though *because* occurs frequently, perhaps because certain speakers are uncertain which of the three possible German conjunctions, *denn, da,* or *weil,* to choose. The occasional use of *unless* may be due to the fact that relatively few speakers seem to feel comfortable using the German "es sei denn, daß" (unless it be [the case] that). Literal translations of correlative conjunctions is fairly common: *beide . . . und* 'both . . . and' [standard German *sowohl . . . wie*], and *nicht nur . . . aber auch* 'not only . . . but also' [rather than *nicht nur . . . sondern auch*].

Mother Tongue and Father Land

CONVENTIONAL WISDOM, which is by no means impervious to error, speaks of the mother tongue as the first language, associated with emotional ties and the experiences of the early, formative years; the fatherland is where one finds oneself through the forces of circumstance and where one must pay the mandatory dues of allegiance. Whether such be the case or not, the fact remains that the communicative behavior inside and outside the private circle of the family and close community often differ dramatically. For speakers who grew up in an era when German was the dominant language of the home and church and English the language of commercial reality, at least some linguistic interference was well-nigh inevitable. The German of the Amana Colonies became exactly what every language must become: a medium of communication that responds to the multiplicity of demands placed upon the speaker by the circumstances of the immediate environment. In the case of Kolonie-Deutsch, its speakers could not avoid the frequent crossing, and with it the eventual obscuring or even obliterating, of the lines of demarcation between the domains of the German and English languages.

A strong sense of self-sufficiency found expression in activities ranging from cultivating the garden to braiding cornhusk rugs. Some products were sold to outside markets for cash. Ultimate reliance, however, was placed upon spiritual values rather than upon any human ability or wisdom.

Amana Society. From *The Amanas Yesterday*, historic photographs collected by Joan Liffring-Zug.

Peter Stuck

3

Amana That Was

A Sense of Community

DURING THE COURSE OF MY RESEARCH, quite a clear picture emerged of life in the Amana Colonies during the period when Kolonie-Deutsch was, without any question whatsoever, the dominant language of the seven villages. Much of what I learned is already documented in the available literature cited in the Bibliography. Two themes, however, need to be stressed more than in previous studies.

The seven villages, operating on a scale that enhances face-to-face contact between individuals, represent a microcosm that can still be grasped in its entirety, even if the macrocosm of the outside world seems at times to defy comprehension. Less prevalent than in earlier years, though far from unknown, is a worldview in which the background, personality, potential, and foibles of each person are understood as part of a coherent and integrated view of the Colonies themselves.

The period of communalism, characterized by a deeply felt sense of *Gemeinschaft* 'community', fostered a familiarity that has since waned in the face of grim and competitive individualism. The result is not only a loss of closeness between individuals and constituencies within the Colonies, but also an erosion of those shared understandings that allowed Colonists to maintain a healthy sense of resilience and assurance in the face of life's vicissitudes. As pointed out later in this chapter, this is perceived by many older residents as a loss by younger Colonists of the capacity to enjoy life spontaneously and with humor.

The link between these two points will become even more evident as we consider what the sources themselves felt needed to be said.

What Is in a Name?

WHAT IS IN A NAME? A great deal more than one might think! It is, after all, one of the first things that we say in addressing another person, and the one thing that is almost always said when talking about a third party. Names, therefore, help to establish the basic context of a conversation: who is talking to whom, and about whom. It is no wonder then that names often carry significance beyond their simple function as proper nouns. Such is certainly the case in the Amana Colonies, where names often become part of the ritual of establishing and reestablishing the rapport that enables speakers to converse freely in Kolonie-Deutsch.

Any person who has spent a lifetime in the seven villages knows just which families have achieved prominence, which enjoy special kinship ties with various other families, which are associated with certain occupational activities, and so forth. In other words, there is an unwritten but clearly understood lexicon of names, particularly surnames, each bearing more information than simply immediate family ties. In earlier years there also developed a fairly well-defined sense of what an acceptable given name might be. Parents who tried to introduce more innovative names may not have gained much credit for their efforts. An unfamiliar given name was often thought of as "ein schrecklicher Name" (a terrible name), "ein amerikanischer Name" (an American name), in short, "kein richtiger Kolonie-Name" (no proper Colony name). To the cognizant, a name will immediately convey some very important information about an individual's background, and about what one presumably might expect from that person.

In this social milieu where it was important—and still possible—to place everyone in a societal taxonomy based on family ties, the custom was perpetuated of regularly referring to a married woman by *die* (the) + maiden name + given name. Though this practice no longer prevails as it once did, a speaker in early midlife made an extra point of explaining that, her married name notwithstanding, she was and continues to be addressed by this formula. The married name may indeed be used, and in the *Inspirations-Historie,* the chronicle of the Community of True Inspiration, one finds such references to women as *die* (the) + married name + feminine ending, as in *die Schäfferin* (Mrs. Schaeffer). At times the married name will be cited in the same formulaic manner as a maiden name (i.e., before the given name), but in these cases, reference is usually to an individual who is well known as "Mrs. So-and-so."[1]

In earlier days, one was (and, to a striking extent, still is) expected to show considerable respect in addressing or referring to older persons. The rule was "immer die Hand geben" (always offer the hand). Less common today, though not altogether abandoned, is the practice of calling all adults of the Colonies *Bruder* 'Brother' and *Schwester* 'Sister'. Even if not used as frequently nowadays, such forms, like the giving of the hand, are felt to be "mehr anständig" (more proper), and it seems that an inextricable link exists between propriety, good taste, and genuine affection.

Hence it was that terms of respect and terms of endearment typically came to be one and the same. An older individual, whether related by kinship ties or not, might be called *Onkel* 'Uncle' or *Dande* (i.e., *Tante*) 'Aunt'. Senior members of the community may still be addressed as *Oma* 'Grandma' or perhaps somewhat less frequently *Opa* 'Grandpa'. One interview subject was delighted to tell about *Oma Henni, Oma Minni,* and *Oma Heinche,* adding that "zu meinen Kindern sind sie alle Oma" (to my children they are all Grandma).

Young or old, Inspirationist or outsider, everyone was eligible for a byname or nickname. The vocabulary itself may be German, such as "der Brillen-Andreas" (Spectacles-Andrew), an itinerant who is said to have dropped his eyeglasses into a container of alcoholic brew, where by chance he found them three weeks later.[2] From yet an earlier period one also hears English nicknames such as Sonny and Half-Pint—the youngest, but not necessarily smallest, son of his family. Perhaps most interesting were the names that supposed fairly fluent bilingualism and often involved light-spirited wordplay. The name *Rohrbacher* literally means 'one coming from the reed stream'; over time the word *Rohr* 'reed' has also come to mean 'tube' or even 'pipe' (i.e., for plumbing). In this manner, one scion of the Rohrbacher family came to be known locally as "Piper."

What is in a name? Not least significantly, it serves as an element that enhances an atmosphere of familiarity and community and in so doing, sets the stage for the true Kolonie-Deutsch conversation.

Life Seen from the Lighter Side

WHILE LIFE AND PRACTICE in the Colonies may have become more liberal over time, the folks living in the seven villages are not necessarily having more *fun* nowadays. When asked what has really changed since 1932, an impressive number of respondents concurred in citing two points: an erosion in the feeling of *Gemeinschaft* 'community'; and the loss of a healthy, spontaneous sense of humor. The two factors are by no means unrelated. I asked several women to tell me about their life in the communal era. Even taking into account the ameliorating effects of selective memory, I was struck by the consistent recollection of the good times that were enjoyed when the demand for many hands to complete arduous but necessary tasks afforded the perfect atmosphere in which to sing, gossip, tease, and generally to enjoy the company of one's peers.

There is so much agreement in the accounts of various sources that one can easily reconstruct the typical day of a young woman in former decades. Rising early in the morning, she prepares to meet her friends and with them joins other small groups headed toward the fields. The work of the day might be gathering and cleaning onions or some other routine job. To offset the sheer monotony of the task, the young women socialize in word and song. Especially after 1932 when meals were no longer taken in the dining halls of communal kitchens, noon meant a break for a picnic lunch of sandwiches and soda pop. Naturally, it takes a bit of effort to get back to work in the afternoon. At some point the field boss comes along and tells the young women to quit singing and get to work. These imperatives that somehow fail to dampen the workers' spirits are granted something resembling due compliance. At the end of the day the women return home, tired but resolved to repeat the cycle another day.

One raconteur maintains that she only experienced something similar in postcommunal times as part of a World War II–era women's work brigade. Other sources give slightly different accounts, but the basic message seems always the same: being together brought enjoyment, "wir haben fun gehabt" (we had fun).

Not surprisingly, such enjoyment in the company of one's peers was not confined to the workplace. One woman vividly recalls German verses that she and her friends sang as they strolled through town on Sunday afternoons to meet other young folks at the train depot. Just as I was getting more involved in her account of the Sunday afternoon outing, the interview subject asked me to turn off the tape recorder so that she could repeat a few lines from one of the songs popular during her adolescent years. These lyrics seemed harmless enough to me. Evidently the words aroused stronger reaction in another era, when this woman's mother forbade her daughter from singing such ditties in public. What intrigued me most about all this was not the source's keen memory for detail (conceded by many to be excellent), nor her desire to maintain propriety so many years later, but rather her expressed purpose of wishing to illustrate the fun-loving spirit of earlier Colony life.

This hankering to enjoy a good time often found harmless expression in the jokes and pranks whose creation seems so effortless to young people. On occasion things may have gone a bit too far, as in the case of a young woman who was told to process a load of potatoes for her communal kitchen. Without thinking about the fact that it was April Fool's Day, she complied, only to find out that the work had not been part of the kitchen boss' plan for the day. Both the perpetrators and object of this prank vividly recall the incident.

Although I interviewed fewer men on the subject of their earlier work lives, the common theme of their recollections proved to be much the same as those of the women: a good time was had by all. A sadly understudied corpus of extant poems celebrates the work experience in lighthearted strains.[3] These include "Das Sunshine Circle Lied" (The Sunshine Circle Song), "Das Mistlied" (The Manure Song), Carl H. Zimmerman's "Das Lied der Fabrick" (The Factory Song), "Ein Gedankenspiel auf der Wachtstube" (Playful Recollections of the Watchtower [literally: on (the topic of) the Watch Room]), "Die Wester Brüder" (The West Amana Brothers), and more.[4] A number of passages from these local creations follow. Their overall tone and purpose are suggested by lines in the middle of "Das Mistlied":

> Es hat ein jeder was zu knurren
> Zu fluchen, schimpfen und zu murren
> Doch sind wir alle muntre Knaben
> Das zeigen uns're dichter Gaben.

> (Everyone has something to growl,
> Curse, complain, or murmer about,
> Still we are all cheerful lads,
> And that is what our poetic gifts show.)

In other words, in a world where there is always some source of aggravation, why not use our talents to rise above negative factors through a healthy infusion of lighthearted humor? Much the same sentiment is expressed by the closing lines of this text.

Dieses Mistlied zu erdenken
Mus[s]ten wir die brains ver[r]enken
Aber hoffen tun wir auch
Das[s] es nicht zum Mis[s]gebrauch
Doch zum Nutzen wird gelesen
Sonst wär' es umsonst gewesen.

(In order to think up this Manure Song
We had to dislocate our brains
But we also hope
That it not be read for misuse
But rather for benefit,
Otherwise it would all have been in vain.)

"Das Lied der Fabrick" also concludes with an expression of the
author's desire that no significance be ascribed to the text beyond an
attempt to view life from the lighter side:

Ich hoffe das[s] ein jeder lacht
Ueber das Lied wo blos[s] vor fun gemacht.

(I hope that everyone will laugh
about the song that was merely made for fun.)

Even though the author claims that this song "was merely made for
fun," the reader cannot altogether dismiss the possibility that verse of
this sort might allow its author(s) to express a form of criticism
otherwise not considered appropriate or even admissible in the social
context of communal Amana. Be that as it may, one still needs to ask
just what sorts of things the speakers of Kolonie-Deutsch did, and still
do, find humorous.

Humor in the German Language

AS IS ONLY NATURAL, speakers of Kolonie-Deutsch are in overwhelming
agreement that jokes told in German are funnier than those told in
English. Apart from an understandable preference for wit in one's first
language, such assertions often pass rather glibly over specific factors
that allow material in one language to strike the hearer differently than

the same or very similar content rendered in another language. It is instructive to probe the salient factors in more detail.

First of all, German idioms may lend themselves more naturally to a particular humorous effect. Coffee is a much-loved beverage in Amana and its sister villages. Those who drink it are not at all shy about commenting on its quality. One poor soul found "das Zeug . . . so schwach, es kann nicht aus der Tasse laufen" (the stuff . . . so weak, it cannot run out of the cup). The point is perfectly comprehensible in English. In German, however, one may use the verb *laufen* 'to run' in far more contexts than in English to describe the motion of fluids. There is a more natural basis for near-personification of the coffee, whose lamentable weakness leaves it unable to "run."

At times local humor presumes familiarity with the specific usage patterns of Kolonie-Deutsch rather than simply of German in general. One speaker invited her neighbor over to hear all the latest news, which amounted to "gräßlich viel Stoff" (gruesomely much stuff). German *gräßlich* 'gruesome[ly]', like English *terribly* or *awfully,* here simply means 'very'. Speakers of Kolonie-Deutsch know that this usage of *gräßlich,* though common enough in local circles, is not considered the hallmark of elegant speech in the standard language. The party who was invited to get an earful of the latest tidbits of local news assured me that the choice of *gräßlich* here added an undeniable air of anticipation and tongue-in-cheek humor to the entire episode.

There have also been countless attempts at enhancing humor through intentional use of forms reflecting the idiosyncracies of Amana German, as in the rules for the *Sängerbund* 'Singers' Association'. In themselves, they appear merely to set up good-natured guidelines for participants' behavior. Speakers of Kolonie-Deutsch find that apart from any inherent humor of their literal content, the very imitation of local pronunciation makes these rules mildly hilarious.

ZEHN VERHANDLUNGSMAASREGLE,
WO SICH DIE SENGER DARNACH RICHDE SOLLE.

1. Net schmohke.
2. Net schnubfe.
3. Net tschuhe; iwwerhaubt net uff'n Bohde schbukke.
4. Net saufe beim Singe; mir kleiche nichderne Kerle.
5. Die Senger solle immer komme am bedreffende Ab'nd.
6. Donnerschdags werd ksunge, weil kein Deich im Schbeißsaal is.
7. Wenn einer von de Senger sein Gebordsdag hat un's werd bei'm

ksunge, derf'r driehde un's derf jeder saufe bis'r umfallt.
8. Schbeckdahkel, Brille, Nauslaufe un Schbeerke is farbode.
9. Kein Senger, wo bsoffe is wenn'r herkommt, derf sein Dullje
   kstehn.
10. Mar soll auch die Schuh un Stiffel abbudse eh mar rinkommt.
    (Die Ruhl do hett eigentlich vorne dran kheert, awwer's is jetz
    so gedruckt.)

(TEN RULES OF BEHAVIOR,
TO WHICH THE SINGERS ARE TO CONFORM

1. Do not smoke.
2. Do not take snuff.
3. Do not chew, and above all, do not spit on the floor.
4. Do not booze while singing; we like sober chaps.
5. The singers should always come on the proper evening.
6. We sing on Thursdays because there is no dough [rising] in the
   dining hall.
7. If one of the singers has his birthday and there is drinking at his
   place, he can treat us and everyone may guzzle until he falls
   over.
8. Uproars, making noise, running outside and courting are
   forbidden.
9. No singer who is drunk upon arrival may admit his depravity.
10. We should also clean off our shoes and boots before we enter.
    (That rule actually belonged at the beginning, but this is how it
    got printed.))

In another instance, a poem frequently read and sung in the
villages, Goethe's "Heidenröslein," is parodied as part of the longer
local-color epic "Die Wester Brüder." The basis of humor lies here in
the playful adaptation of a famous text, familiar to virtually anyone
literate in German, to local situations. The famous rose of Goethe's
poem is now the blossoming young Rose of a village family.

> Arno sah ein Röslein steh'n,
> Dort in Scheuner's Küchen.
> Arno sprach, "Ich will mal seh'n
> Ob ich die kann pflücken."
> Sagte er sehr leis zu sich,
> "Ach könnt' ich diese Ros doch pflücken,
> Das würde mich beglücken."

Da versuchte er sein Glück
Und sie wies ihn nicht zurück.
Kaum ein Jahr wird noch verstreichen
Bis sie sich die Hände reichen,
Um fortan auf dieser Erden,
Treu sich Mann und Frau zu werden.

(Arno saw a little Rose standing
There in Scheuner's kitchen,
Arno said, "I'd like to see once
Whether I can pluck it."
Softly said he to himself,
"Ah, if I could but pluck this rose,
That would make me happy."
So he tried his luck,
And she did not send him away.
Hardly a year will pass by
Until they give their hands in marriage,
And evermore upon this earth
Be loyal man and wife.)

With evidence of such playful creativity, it is no wonder that a tradition of declamation (*das Deklamieren*) blossomed, and for many years no marriage reception, anniversary, or other festivity was quite complete without an appropriate virtuoso performance. A speaker known for her unfeigned reactions to situations good and bad recalled these performances and virtually crooned, "Oh that used to be *wonderful.*" Even those without special talent enjoyed producing a good turn of phrase: "das haben wir gern getan." (We liked doing that.) Though older texts such as those cited in this chapter are only rarely resurrected, a new tradition of creating and sharing locally created verse has been inaugurated in the form of the annual poetry evening sponsored by the Amana Arts Guild. It is significant that texts have been read at this poetry evening in both English and German. Not all texts are humorous.

AMANA

EPILOGUE OR PROLOGUE

S'nimmt nich mehr lang, wen alles ist vergessen.
Die Gräber Steinen lehnen krummer schon.
An vielen kan man kaum der Namen lesen,

der Wind und Regen hat gewisch't davon.
Das Gotteshaus steh't da so leer und leise.
Kein' Dienstlied schallet van darinnen 'raus.
Was einmal was so brünstig und so heisse
    ist eben still—das Lied is nunmehr aus.
Nun fremde Hände schmicken jetz die Gräber.
Zum andacht wird es meistens nur getan.
Es sindt bloss übrig einsame Aufhebern
    die niemals glaubten sicherlich daran.
Leer steh't der Saal, der Friedhof ist verlassen;
Ein kalt' Museum mitten in der Welt.
Kann's sein das hier auf diesen schönen Gassen
    die Inspiration sich wieder neu erhöll't?

—GLENN H. WENDLER (1990)

(It won't take much longer, until everything is forgotten.
The gravestones are already leaning more crookedly.
On many one can barely read the names,
    the wind and rain have wiped them away.
The House of God stands there so empty and still.
No song or worship rings out from within.
What once was so fervent and ardent
    Is now quiet—the song is over.
Now strange hands decorate the graves.
Now it is mostly done only out of piety.
There are just a few lonesome caretakers left
    who never really firmly embraced the faith.
The sanctuary stands empty, the cemetery has been abandoned;
It is a cold museum in the middle of the world.
Can it be that here on these fair lanes
    Inspiration will dawn once again?)

Especially insightful was the observation that in earlier days humor consisted more of anecdotes than of jokes. Indeed, in older humorous texts one does encounter a rather frequent and unabashed reference to the joys and sorrows, the foibles and frailties, of well-known individuals. The lessons may have universal application as in many a joke, but the content of the material is focused on the commissions and omissions of real-life acquaintances, as in the typical anecdote. Hence, even though there is seldom any actual narrative content, the stanzas of a poem such as "Die Wester Brüder" take on a near-anecdotal tone in their reference to familiar personalities. Because these older humorous texts (many dating from the earliest decades of our century) are not readily accessible to modern readers, I have tried to share a representative sampling.

> Der August Griess ist unser Bäcker,
> Und nebenbei noch Apotheker,
> Und trägt er gleich kein Doktorhut,
> Doch seine Mittel wirken gut.

> (August Griess is our baker,
> And on the side also our druggist,
> And even though he has no doctorate,
> His remedies work well.)

Many of the vignette portraits of this poem are pointed references to the weaknesses of village residents.

> Der Georg Bortz ist kugelrund,
> Er wiegt mehr denn 200 Pfund!
> So hör nun Jack und lasz dir sagen,
> Ich möcht Dein Bäuchlein auch nicht tragen.
> Geholfen kann noch werden Dir,
> Trink Essig anstatt homemade Bier!

> (George Bortz is round as a ball,
> He weighs more than 200 pounds!
> So listen, Jack, and let me tell you,
> I wouldn't like to carry around your belly either.
> You can be helped, however:
> Drink vinegar instead of homemade beer!)

Familiarity may prompt teasing. It also stimulates compassion, as in a stanza devoted to a man in West Amana whose life bore the imprint of personal tragedy.

> Der Bruder Flick ist Schlosserbaas
> Der einstmals eine Frau besasz,
> Die aber nun im Graben ruht
> Doch drob verliert er nicht den Mut.

> (Brother Flick is the chief mechanic
> Who once had a wife
> Who, however, now rests in the grave —
> Still, despite that, he has not lost courage.)

Each cultural milieu exhibits a preference for certain themes in its corpus of indigenous humor. In the Amana Colonies (at least in the older texts), two prominent and recurrent topics are dirt and drinking. The author of the poem "Ein Gedankenspiel auf der Wachtstube," dedicated to the adventures in the "Wachtstube," refuses to beat around the bush:

> Am schnellsten käm ich wohl zum Zweck
> Wenn ich beschreiben tät den Dreck
>
> (I would get to the point the fastest
> If I would describe the filth.)

Conditions in the watchtower are shameful. "Läuse krabbeln auf dem Kissen." (Lice crawl on the [watchman's] pillow.) Anyone peeking inside would surely conclude "es wär ein Haus für Schwein" (it was a house for swine).

No dirt, of course, holds the fascination of excrement. A man has not attained full development if he has failed to master the craft of working with the end product of his livestock. Those who shy away from such work are regarded with disdain. The chief of cattle operations in West Amana is distinguished by, among other things, his active involvement in this area of enterprise. In "Die Wester Brüder" we read,

> Schoenfelder Carl, der Kuhbaas ist,
> Der hat gar viel zu tun mit Mist.
>
> (Carl Schoenfelder, who is the cow boss,
> He has a lot to do with manure.)

On the other hand, there are those who are decried in "Das Mistlied" for their lack of expertise and interest in this vital activity.

> Dennoch gibt's mancher Separatist
> Der nicht 'mal weisz was Kuhmist ist.
> Sie denken in der Stille bei sich
> Das Mist Fahr'n geht auch ohne mich.
>
> (Still, there is many a Separatist [i.e., Inspirationist]
> Who doesn't even know what cow manure is,
> They think in private to themselves:
> Hauling manure will go on without me.)

The other topic that recurs with some striking frequency is the excessive consumption of alcohol. In "Die Wester Brüder" we gain some idea of the long-standing tongue-in-cheek recognition of this problem:

> Im Schulhauskeller ist es schön
> Da liegt der Saft der Reben.
> Dort tut der Gustav Schädlich steh'n
> Und Wester Wein uns geben.
> Doch der Gustav wird, oh weh,
> Jetzt mit seinem Wein sehr zäh.
> Letztes Jahr, so hört man murren
> Sind die Reben uns erfroren.
> Man sagte es war Gottes Will'
> Den manche tranken gar zu viel.

> (In the schoolhouse cellar it is beautiful,
> There lies the juice of the grapes.
> There Gustav Schädlich stands
> Giving us West Amana Wine.[5]
> But, alas, Gustav is becoming
> Tough about [dispensing] his wine.
> Last year, so we hear folks murmur,
> The grapes froze for us.
> They say it was the will of God,
> Because some were drinking far too much.)

All this does not mean that the good folks of Amana remain oblivious of the other great subject of folk humor—the life-engendering processes. Though I did not seek it, I was braced by past experience in other ethnic enclaves for a barrage of unique lore on this topic. I did indeed encounter some such material, though not as much as anticipated. One story that is so familiar that it was even published in the newspaper *Willkommen* involves an outsider who chanced upon an unusually large funeral procession. Upon asking who the deceased was, the visitor was told that the departed had been one of the Colonies' best *Brüder* 'brothers'. In the typical pronunciation of Kolonie-Deutsch, the dead man had been one of the community's best *Brieder,* a virtual homonym of English *breeder.* Being unfamiliar with the finer points of Amana German, the stranger could only gaze at the many individuals in attendance and take the informative Colonist at his word.[6]

Conversation with residents of the seven villages continues today

to be a pleasant activity, seldom devoid of benevolent joviality. Much
of the richest humor, however, recalls the more distant past. With the
end of communalism there appears to have been a waning of a certain
lightheartedness that is an overlooked and underappreciated legacy of
traditional Colony life. Ties of familiarity were weakened and with
that, no doubt, the sense of intimacy felt by so many speakers to be an
essential requirement for active use of Amana German. In the end, this
has meant a deterioration of the emotional vigor required for continued
use of Kolonie-Deutsch as a vital language, sustained by the spontaneous use of a community of active speakers.

Village Voices

ALTHOUGH SOME OF THE SEVEN VILLAGES enjoy special preeminence
because of a particular historical landmark or other attraction for
outside visitors, the collective term "Amana Colonies," with an
emphasis in popular literature on a shared communal heritage, might
suggest that the earlier history of the Colonies was one characterized
by a good deal of close interaction and sharing between the villages. As
a matter of fact, such was not necessarily the case. Prior to the Change
of 1932, each village was operated independently, with its own Council
of Elders exercising final authority in temporal and spiritual affairs.
More than one source with an interest in local history has suggested
during interview sessions that the earlier eldership consciously
attempted to foster individual patterns of community life within the
respective settlement centers, so that local residents would not feel
drawn toward too much potentially disquieting contact across village
lines. Whether such was indeed the case or not, the perception persists
that each village maintains a distinct character that was already well
established decades ago.[7]

This idea is expressed in a number of ways. When one closely
considers the life patterns of the seven villages, "man merkt doch ein
bißl Unterschied" (one does indeed notice a bit of difference), albeit to
a less striking degree than in earlier years. I asked approximately half
of my interview subjects whether such differences do in fact exist, and
if so, what their nature might be. The typical response was one
affirming the distinct character of the various centers of settlement,
while finding it difficult to identify specific, salient features of life in

the individual villages. One good-natured Colonist, who allowed me to press insistently for details that would illustrate the situation, finally stated that there was "vielleicht nichts da, wo man gerade den Finger darauf tun kann" (perhaps nothing there that one could exactly put a finger on), but insisted emphatically that "etwas ist ein bißchen anders . . . ich täte sagen, das ist immer noch merkwürdig [bemerkenswert]" (something is a bit different . . . I would say that that [factor] is still worth noting).

Yet persistence brings its reward. More than once an individual who initially claimed s/he could not describe the unique nature of the villages returned to the topic in later conversations. One Colonist of few but sagacious words concluded after reflection that a key factor is the sense of local pride. Most Colonists could not be expected to remain objective about their home villages, and the inquisitive outsider would need "to ask folks about other villages—not their own." A married couple who consented to a common interview showed visible delight at the prospect of being able to discuss this topic, not least of all because they were originally from different villages and evidently loved to remind each other, after some six decades of marriage, of that fact. The husband noted, "Die Dörfer haben gedacht, o, wir sind die Besten, die Homesteader haben gedacht, wir denken, wir sind vielleicht ein bißl besser . . ." (The villages thought, oh, we're the best, the Homestead folks thought, we think we're maybe a little better . . .), only to have his wife interject with teasing laughter "Ja, aber *wir* haben's gewußt" (Yes, but *we* knew [that we were better]), to which the husband responded, "Wir waren also aber auch sicher" (But we, too, were certain of it). Perhaps some individuals do find it difficult to give a specific and objective description of the villages, and perhaps some simply find it difficult to remain objective in giving a specific description!

Those with a bent toward the historic explanation of things often refer to the importance of differing attitudes toward adoption of the English language. South Amana, with two railroad lines—the Milwaukee in Upper South Amana and the Rock Island in Lower South Amana—enjoyed a particular sense of mobility, and its residents are reputed to have learned English faster and better than most Colonists. Evidently a similar situation prevailed in Homestead, located on a major thoroughfare, and in Amana, known in local parlance as Main Amana, where there was also a railroad station and industry dependent upon clients living outside the Colonies. Residents of the remaining villages (East, Middle, High, and West Amana) may, in general, have been a bit slower in switching to the use of English.

A more important issue than differences in the use of English is the variety in the German of the seven villages. Intriguing as the topic is, we can at best hope to capture indications of patterns that may still be discernible but were significantly more pronounced at an earlier period than they are today. In great part, we are dealing with linguistic vestiges of the Amana that was.

My first information on the existence of microdialects within the Amana Colonies came from an older man who was recounting earlier work experiences. While serving on a dredge crew, he noted that "je weiter hinauf [wir] gegangen sind gegen den Rapids zu, da haben sie einen anderen Dialekt gesprochen" ([we noticed that] as we went further up toward the rapids, they spoke a different dialect). Another speaker noted that characteristic village speech patterns were "arg pronounced" (awfully pronounced) during her childhood, and attributed the decline of these variations to the integration of children into schools that now draw pupils from more than a single village. Be that as it may, older residents concur that the speakers in East and Main Amana spoke an especially striking form of Kolonie-Deutsch, and "die Mittler ganz besonders jetzt noch" (especially, even now, the residents of Middle Amana).

The blurring of earlier speech boundaries does not mean that the existence of the dialects is being forgotten. The first phase of our tape archive project concluded with an evening program featuring an open forum of discussion with residents of the seven villages. During this meeting an appeal was made to those in attendance for suggestions of topics that might provide thematic foci for future interviews and/or give direction to the research efforts of the project staff. A gentleman whom I later interviewed and who, I subsequently discovered, is blessed with an unusual sensitivity to issues of language and communication stood up and encouraged us to pursue an interest that we had expressed, in admittedly rather casual terms, in varieties of German within the Colonies. This suggestion by a local resident, that greater attention be paid to village microdialects, appeared to gain the spontaneous concurrence of the other speakers of Kolonie-Deutsch in attendance.

To illustrate his points, the speaker offered a concrete example for our consideration. When fishing in the local canal, an Amana resident "sets" the throw-lines, just as one "sets" a trap. When speaking in German, however, one rarely uses the verb *setzen* 'to set' for this activity. (I have encountered only one person who reported isolated use of *setzen* in this context.) Rather, the prevailing expression is either "die Lines legen" (to lay the lines), perhaps on analogy with "die Angel legen" (to lay the hook) or "die Lines stellen" (to place the lines). What, this speaker of Kolonie-Deutsch asked, is correct German? Even more to the point: should one attribute this multiplicity of idiomatic forms primarily to differences of geography, social environment, age, or perhaps simply to spontaneous local invention? As this member of the audience outlined his questions, it was abundantly evident that he had caught the rapt attention of his fellow Colonists. He also convinced me that there are speakers of Kolonie-Deutsch who have given unsuspectedly sophisticated thought to questions of language use.

An issue that must be carefully addressed at some point is that of the origins of the village dialects. Many Colonists have traveled to Germany. More than a few return with tales of having encountered native Germans who speak virtually "the same" dialect, or so it would seem. This is especially true for those who visit the German state of Hesse; to a lesser extent, this has also been true for individuals visiting sites in Saxony, something that will undoubtedly prove much easier to do since reunification of the German nation. It would seem natural enough to assume that some of the varieties of Kolonie-Deutsch have their roots in the regional dialects of the fatherland.

The one specifically dialectological study carried out in the Colonies—admittedly on a limited sampling of the speaker-pool but nevertheless with great thoroughness—centered on speakers whose German is demonstrably Hessian in origin.[8] Other speech patterns with vestiges of European dialect characteristics have received only a limited amount of the attention that they deserve.

Many speakers are quick to point out, however, that while Kolonie-Deutsch may embrace elements traceable to specific areas in Germany, the local microdialects as such did develop in the United States. While some villages may have had large representations from a specific region in Germany (see the following discussion), not all families were able to settle alongside others who shared a common region of origin in the European homeland. Young Inspirationists married into families of different backgrounds, and as a result many local residents can claim grandparents with two, three, or even four distinct regions of origin. According to this point of view, Kolonie-Deutsch is an amalgamation of original dialects, with specific features that gained currency primarily in the setting of the Amana Colonies.

Two sources expressed the opinion that village microdialects developed in response to the influential speech patterns of local teachers. This point merits consideration. Despite abundant untapped source material, we know far too little about early education in the Colonies. Schoolchildren, whose social contacts focused primarily on the home village, may well have emulated the language of their teachers more vigorously than might nowadays be expected when social mobility and mass communication are unthinkingly assumed.

Finally, one does encounter a few Kolonie-Deutsch speakers who are rather less aware of continental German dialects and who hence espouse no particular view on the origin of local speech varieties. Such individuals, though present, constitute a distinct minority of the sources interviewed. It is quite common to encounter a statement such as the self-abnegating "wir haben immer gedacht, wir wären die Ausnahme" (we [speakers of our village dialect] always thought we were the exception [for having such an unusual variety of German]). Such statements often appear to be fairly formulaic and are often accompanied by an apologetic explanation of how the speaker, as a child, acquired a form of German influenced by the dialect of a parent or grandparent from the continental homeland. It definitely came as a surprise, therefore, to hear a well-educated speaker admit that she only recently read "daß in Deutschland jede Gegend ihren eigenen Dialekt hat, und daß wenn sie aber mit Fremden schwätzen, tun sie Hochdeutsch [sprechen], weil das alle verstehen . . . und das habe ich nicht gerade gewußt" (that in Germany, each region has its own dialect, however, when they speak with strangers, they speak High German, because they all understand that . . . and I just didn't know that).

Whatever the origins of the village dialects, many a speaker is unflinchingly proud to say "ich schwätze gerade wie mir der Schnabel gewachsen ist" (I speak just the way my beak has grown [i.e., as is most natural for me]). It would then seem that if someone were to arrive in Amana speaking in a manner that departed too far from accepted norms, s/he would be made to sense that fact. In some cases this appears to have led to conscious efforts at linguistic acculturation. One individual recalls a grandfather originally from Bavaria, an area sparsely represented in the settlement history of the Amana Colonies, getting together with other Bavarians in an effort to develop pronunciation patterns more like these of other Amana residents: "Die sind als abends zusammengekommen, und dann haben sie gepracticed, da[mit] sie auch so schwätzen könnten wie die Leute in Amana . . . ja, sie wollten doch auch den Dialekt haben, den die Leute in Amana haben." (They sometimes got together in the evenings, and then they practiced so that they could also talk like the people in Amana . . . yes, they also wanted to have the dialect that the people in Amana have.)

No fewer than four sources volunteered recollections, or recollections of the accounts of others, that even the Swiss, whose German often bears the seemingly ineradicable imprint of the speaker's origin, made efforts to approach the locally prevailing linguistic norm: "Die Schweizer haben sich angepaßt, ja, die Schweizer haben sich angepaßt." (The Swiss accommodated, yes, the Swiss accommodated [to the linguistic norm].) One lifetime resident of the Colonies, familiar with Inspirationist history through careful work as a translator of the group's chronicles, pointed out that some Swiss Inspirationist families had already been in the German state of Hesse up to as long as three decades before departing for the United States and, in certain respects, may already have become more German than Swiss.[9] These Inspirationists would have migrated to Germany in the early nineteenth century. I have not been able to determine whether their descendants were among the "Swiss" recalled by my interview subjects and/or their sources. In at least one instance, the Swiss speaker in question would appear to have left Switzerland not long before coming to Amana.[10]

In more recent times, German war brides have brought the Colonists into contact with still other varieties of German. I have not encountered any compelling evidence, however, that the presence of these native speakers of European German has had any dramatic influence on the forms or usage patterns of Kolonie-Deutsch.

Although vestiges of village dialects evident in earlier decades do still exist, their study is complicated by several major factors. The number of verifiable speakers has diminished, and even those identified by other Colonists as "good" sources for the speech of a particular village often admit that increased contact with speakers from other villages and decreased reliance upon German as the primary language have contributed to an erosion of their dialect.

The modest sketch given in this chapter is intended primarily to illustrate ways in which varieties of language ultimately fit into larger patterns of differentiation in social organization and community life. It is not intended to approach a definitive analysis. My hope is that material provided here will stimulate scholars with interest and expertise in dialect studies to set up research programs in the Amana

Colonies. What one encounters are elements of a Central German
Hessian with Franconian and Saxon elements and evidence of southern
(particularly Swabian) influences.[11] An excellent beginning would be
to document responses to a standard questionnaire designed to elicit
forms that identify localized speech patterns. One basis for such work
might be a database of responses to queries such as those of the so-
called "Wenker sentences" (die Wenkersätze) or their equivalent.[12] The
opportunity to do so, with the prospect of obtaining even the most
cautiously qualified results, will not continue to present itself very
much longer!

Amana

THE RESIDENTS OF MAIN AMANA (founded in 1855) are known among
speakers of Kolonie-Deutsch as the Amanaer, or occasionally the
Amaniten.[13] They are also frequently called die Sachsen 'the Saxons'.
Although the historical record shows that Saxons settled throughout the
Colonies and even today one encounters as many or more speakers with
Saxon-influenced speech patterns in Middle as in Main Amana, the fact
remains that the Saxon Inspirationists have been associated over time
with Main Amana.[14] The story still circulates today of a day laborer,
who during the communal period was called to task by the church
eldership for an unbecoming lack of sobriety. When asked where he
had gained access to immoderate quantities of alcohol, the man
responded, "Das sag' ich nicht, den Namen sag' ich nicht, sie wohnen
im Sachsenviertel in der Gurkenstraße." (I won't tell, I won't tell the
name, they live in the Saxon quarter in the Gurkenstraße ['Pickle
Street' in Main Amana].)[15]

Though not invariably associated with inebriation, the Saxons are
proud to claim a reputation as "Helle" (bright folks) and "muntere
Leute" (jolly people) who are wont to cite the wisdom of an old folk
song that tells us this: "Sachsen sind lustige Brüder / sie singen lustige
Lieder" (Saxons are fun-loving brothers / they sing fun-loving songs).
For the most part, this characterization appears to be reasonably
accurate.

Inspirationist history in Germany immediately prior to the
migration to America focuses on the Ronnenburg estate northeast of
Frankfurt, in the province of Hesse; it stands as a matter of historical

record, however, that sect leader Christian Metz did travel to Saxony.[16] Accounts of Colonists with access to family histories point to a number of small centers of the faith in the area roughly bounded by Zwickau and Chemnitz. While further research is desperately needed, it seems fairly certain that one point of concentration within this general area was the cluster of small towns with place-names ending in *-grün*, such as Rittersgrün and Friedrichsgrün. Certain occupational categories were prominently represented among the immigrant Saxons, including mining and the craft trades. (The *Weihnachtspyramide*, or Christmas Pyramid, a traditional craft item from Saxony, has long been a part of customary Christmas celebrations in the Colonies.) The fact that so many local residents with Saxon ties cite a peak in immigration to America around 1880 raises the question whether the decision to leave Germany might not have occurred as part of a much broader reaction to Bismarck's repressive attitudes toward labor in this period.[17]

While association with coreligionists may have played a role in stimulating Saxon migration to the Amana Colonies, an appreciable number of individuals stated without any demurring whatsoever that their forebears were primarily seeking economic opportunity. In some cases social acquaintance with emigrant Inspirationists, rather than any active affiliation with or intense loyalty to the Community of True Inspiration, prompted disaffected Saxon families to leave the European fatherland and seek their fortune in the Colonies.

Among speakers of strong Saxon background—though by no means exclusively in such circles—one is more likely to hear *Kinder* 'children' and *anders* 'otherwise' pronounced as *Kinner* and *anners*; *Bilder* 'pictures' and *älter* 'older' are frequently pronounced as *Biller* and *äller*. In more technical terms, medial alveolar stops are assimilated to preceding homorganic continuants. *Mutter* 'mother' is regularly pronounced *Mudder* and *Stücke* 'pieces' as *Stigge*. Intervocalic voiceless stops are voiced, especially [t] to [d] and [k] to [g]. The verbs *fragen* 'to ask' and *sagen* 'to say' rhyme with *machen* 'to make'. The intervocalic [g] of standard German regularly appears in this dialect as a velar fricative.[18] The vowel [o] is pronounced as [a] before [r] + [d], as in *ardentlich* for *ordentlich* 'orderly' or *warden* for *[ge]worden,* past participle of *werden* 'to become'. The verb *darf / dürfen* 'to be allowed' is often pronounced as derf / derfen, as it is in certain other linguistic circles within the Colonies. The numbers *vierzehn* 'fourteen' and *vierzig* 'forty' are frequently pronounced *verzehn* and *verzig*.

Although a few Colonists recall use of *knepperen* 'to speak' by

earlier Saxon immigrants who were the parents of some of today's
older speakers, I have not encountered spontaneous use of this word in
my own research. In a single instance in another circle of speakers, I
documented the form *nepren* 'to speak'. Finally, although it is not
specifically Saxon, the usual word for 'jelly' in Main Amana is
Schmiersel (a shibboleth whose significance to the village dialects will
soon become clear).

It must be borne in mind that these observations are just that.
There are no "pure" speakers of any Saxon dialects in Amana or in any
of the other villages of the Amana Colonies, and recent literature on
modern German dialects suggests that one might as easily encounter
many of these "Saxon" speech patterns in neighboring dialect regions.[19]

Middle

EVEN THOUGH ONE DOES HEAR references to "Middle Amana," the
official name of this village founded in 1861 is Middle, Iowa; the
German form is *Mittel,* and those who live there are the *Mittler.* I was
not far into my investigation when Colonists began pulling me aside to
give me a confidential earful of what I needed to know about folks
from Middle. Typical remarks included the observation "die waren
immer ein bißl ausbunt, ein bißl frech" (they were always a bit cocky,
a bit fresh). Rather less subtle was the assertion "die Mittler waren die
Schlimmsten" (the folks from Middle were the worst). My own
experiences in this village have left me with far more positive impressions of the folks who live there.[20]

Some would claim that the most salient characteristic of Middle
speech is the pronunciation of words such as *Heim* 'home', *weinen* 'to
cry', or *zwei* 'two' with rounded vowels, as *Heum, weunen,* and *zweu.*
Though some individuals disclaim any familiarity with such pronunciations, anecdotes circulate to illustrate the ways in which speakers of
Middle Kolonie-Deutsch have perpetuated this pronunciation under a
variety of circumstances. One account involves a native of Middle who
was taking a group of visitors on a bus tour through the Colonies. As
the tourists deboarded at one point, the tourguide was heard telling the
visitors in English, presumably influenced by the Middle pronunciation
of certain German vowels, to keep moving since they only had "foyv

minutes toym" until they needed to be back on board the bus. The source for this story has proven herself unusually reliable, but even if the tale were perchance apocryphal, it reflects the common perception that the vestiges of the Middle dialect simply cannot be eradicated, even by switching to a different language.

A less kind account involved a young girl whose pronunciation of *Stock* 'pole' and *Stein* 'stone' was *Tschock* and *Tschein* (metathesis of the elements [š] and [t] of the initial consonant cluster). An aunt from Middle volunteered to help the girl with her speech, only to be told after a short while that pronunciations of *Stohck* with the lengthened vowel heard in the speech of some speakers from Middle and *Steun* with the rounded vowel characteristic of the Middle dialect was not really much improvement at all!

What I have encountered is not only vocalic rounding, but also a genuine uncertainty on the part of some speakers as to which forms are dialect and which are standard German. This is not really so surprising. One older woman from Middle resolved, to my regret, that she would try to speak "good" German with me—that is, with this chap who had had his training in School German. For the most part she did avoid pronunciations that were patently characteristic of her village. In the middle of a narrative sequence she stopped and wondered aloud whether *heut*[e] 'today' were dialect or not. She pronounced it alternatingly as *heut,* then as *heit,* and then again as *heut.* Finally, she concluded that *heut* was dialect, and *heit* the correct form. As a matter of fact, *heute* is the standard German form. But since most speakers of Kolonie-Deutsch, including most in Middle, unround the vowel and pronounce it as *heit*[e], it is no wonder that this individual, already sensitized to the confusion of these vowels, feared that the less prevalent pronunciation must surely be the nonstandard one.

A frequently mentioned shibboleth that divides speakers of the various local dialects is *die Schnake* 'mosquito', locally *die Schnage,* pronounced in some villages as *die Schnoge* and likewise *schlafen* 'to sleep' as *schlofen.* Although I heard both forms from purported "good speakers" of Middle Kolonie-Deutsch, the pronunciation *Schnoge* and *schlofen* predominated. One particularly well-informed speaker reported in correspondence: "My perception is that *schlafen* is more common in Middle than *schlofen.* Incidentally, my use of *schlofen*—and that of other Mittlers as well—was reserved for times when a slightly derogatory connotation was intended, as in 'jetz schloft 'r schonn widder' (now he's asleep *again*!)."

One pronunciation that appears to have been exclusively character-istic of Middle was that of *der Kaffee* 'coffee' as *Keffee* or even *Keffie*, with a strong stress accent on the short vowel of the initial syllable.

Among the words characteristic of Middle speech, none is more often cited than *die Aldan* 'porch', pronounced with strongly fronted vowels. Although a few speakers from other villages admit having used the term, usually as *Altan* or *Aldan* with lower back vowels, the status of this word as a dialect marker associated with Middle was more or less canonized as such when it was used in the heritage celebration play, *This Song is for the Fleeting Days,* written by Emilie Hoppe in 1986 and produced in 1988.[21] Nowadays, most sources are prone to recall having made fun of the folks from Middle and their lexicon: "Ich habe in Amana gewohnt und wir haben immer gelacht über die Mittler, sie haben Wörter gehabt . . . wir haben die Halle gesagt, outside porch oder was wir [gehabt] haben . . . und sie haben gesagt die Aldan . . . und wir haben immer gelacht wenn sie gesagt haben . . . die Aldan, und ihre Zunge war gerade ein bißchen anders." (I lived in [Main] Amana and we always laughed about the people from Middle, they had [their own] words . . . we said *die Halle, outside porch,* or whatever we had . . . and they said *die Aldan* . . . and we always laughed when they said . . . *die Aldan,* and their tongue was just a bit different.)

Although a certain pronunciation of this word may identify the speaker as a native of Middle, its use as an item of active vocabulary does not. During a visit to the Ebenezer community in New York, Christian Metz witnessed a flood and wrote back to Amana "so stieg das Wasser höher und höher und kam zuletzt auf die Altan von unserem Hause" (so the water rose higher and higher and eventually came onto the porch [*die Altan*] of our house).[22] The letter dates from 1861, the year in which Middle was founded. It is tempting to speculate that Metz may have acquired the term from active involvement with the folks who established that village. At the moment, however, such speculation must remain exactly that and no more.

Other typical terms include *Schillee* or even *Schillie* for 'jelly' (a shibboleth whose reliability has been questioned) and *Madde* rather than *Quark* for a cultured milk product sometimes marketed in this country as "yoghurt cheese." I received something less than unanimity of opinion, though an appreciably strong indication, that for some speakers from Middle the usual term for taking peas out of their shell is *schoten* 'to shell' or *Schoten tepsen/töpsen* 'pop the shells' (usually pronounced *schudden* or *Schudden tepsen*) rather than *Erbsen ausmachen* 'take out the peas'. Most speakers noted that there are two terms for a kitchen paring knife, *das Ristmesser* and *das Schälmesser*. Persons from Middle seemed to favor *Ristmesser,* but isolated individuals preferred *Schälmesser.*

In sum, my impression was that the microdialect of Middle probably was—and indeed still is—the most strikingly characteristic within the Colonies. It is most often cited by residents of other villages as an example of language variation within the Colonies, and the speakers from Middle themselves are among the most eager to discuss their own dialect. I would urge any investigators hoping to work in the villages to place the *Mittler* high on the list of sources to be approached.

East Amana

THOUGH ONLY A FEW MINUTES BY CAR from Main Amana, East Amana is, in a sense, an idyllic retreat far removed from the other villages.[23] There are no commercial establishments open to the public or a separate post office, though both once existed; there is nowhere to go from East Amana except out into the country. It is perhaps the serenest of the settlements. Appropriately enough, East Amana was originally founded in 1860 as an outpost for sheepherding.[24]

Both longtime residents and others cite the sense of close-knit community in East Amana. In earlier days the post office building housed a sewing machine used for preparing the *Totenkleider* or 'death clothes' for the deceased, and work uniforms for the *Tagelöhner* or 'day wage earners', the ubiquitous outsiders whose labor augmented the capacity of the Colonies' work force. Needless to say, such an environment offered a natural locus for the exchange of the most diverse bits of news.

Operated on a human scale that has always fostered face-to-face contact, East Amana still maintains the air of modesty and unpretentiousness that long caused it to be called "Ost, wo's nichts kost" (East [Amana], where it doesn't cost [anything to live]).

All closeness and cohesiveness notwithstanding, East has the distinction of once having been the center of activity by an ethnic enclave within an enclave, as it were. One frequently encounters recollections such as "in Ost war nichts wie Böhmen" (in East Amana

there were nothing but Bohemians). During the earlier years of this
century, there evidently were a number of Czech-Americans living
"behind" East Amana (as one resident put it), outside the territory
communally owned by the Inspirationists. These so-called "Bohemians"
from Cedar Rapids and surrounding communities seem to have had a
certain preference for making purchases and doing other business in
East Amana. Several sources have hinted, not necessarily in any
unkindly manner, that the presence of the "Bohemians" was still one
more factor that set East Amana a bit apart from the other villages.
This aspect of local ethnographic history deserves further investigation.

With their actual or perceived removal from the mainstream of
Colony traffic, it is not surprising that the residents of East Amana
developed speech patterns felt by some to be among the most distinctive
of village dialects. One speaker from East Amana summarized the two
characteristics most frequently cited: a long [o:] in place of standard
German long [a:] (*Schnoge* for *Schnage* 'mosquito', *schlofen* for
schlafen 'to sleep', etc.), and the less vigorous pronunciation of [r]
(actually, vocalization of postvocalic [r] with resultant lengthening of
the preceding vowel). "Es war ein Unterschied in der Sprache . . . in
Ost, wir haben . . . die [elongated] *O* gesagt . . . wir haben nicht der
R gesagt: Kahl [Karl]" (There was a difference in the language . . . in
East, we . . . said the [elongated] *O* . . . we didn't say the *R*: Kahl
[instead of Karl]).

The speakers from East Amana seem to have accepted their dialect
without too much ado. One lifetime resident said it was simply
understood that as far as the speech of her village was concerned,
spelling and pronunciation did not agree: "*Schaf* wird's geschrieben,
Schof wird's gesprochen." (It is written *Schaf* 'sheep' and pronounced
Schof.) One wry observer noted that the folks from East Amana
provided other Colonists with an occasional source of humor, for
instance in pronouncing *Bratwurst* 'bratwurst, fried sausage' as
Brotwurst [literally 'bread sausage'].

I did find some East Amana speakers with the vocalic rounding of
the sort discussed in connection with the Middle dialect, and also
evidence of the near-universal unrounded vowel in *heit*[e] for *heute*.
Most individuals also tend to pronounce *Tante* 'aunt' as *Dande,* as is
true virtually throughout the villages. These and other pronunciation
features appeared, however, to be as much, and often possibly more,
a case of ideolect, individual or idiosyncratic speech patterns, as a part
of any prevalent village dialect. Older sources, those over eighty years

of age who were young adults at the time of the 1932 Change, still tended to associate East Amana with the Colonies' Hessian legacy. One contact referred quite intentionally to the speech of that village as *Hessisch* 'Hessian'. Although my own study was not primarily one of dialectology, I would have to agree in general terms that the Hessian element is certainly present.[25]

Homestead

HOMESTEAD IS A BIT UNUSUAL in several ways. Established in 1861, it is located on land lying outside the territory purchased when the Inspirationists first moved to Iowa.[26] Like South Amana, it is located on U.S. Route 6, a major east-west highway, at the intersection of a state highway leading from Interstate 80 to the Amana Colonies. Not surprisingly, Homestead is credited with being one of the more cosmopolitan and outward-looking of the settlement centers.

Many a Colonist volunteered comments such as "die Homesteader gleichen ihren eigenen Weg zu gehen" (the Homesteaders like to go their own way), that they consider themselves to be "vornehme Leute" (distinguished people), or that they like to speak "ein bißl mehr fancy Deutsch" (a bit more fancy German). Surprising to me was the fact that no Homesteader ever seemed to show the blush of modesty (in my presence, at least) at hearing such assertions.

Homestead is also the one single village whose speech has been the specific focus of a fair amount of scholarly attention. Barbara Selzer's 1941 M.A. thesis dealt virtually exclusively with the language of her home village.[27] Kurt Rein has provided an excellent study of the Homestead dialect, based on fieldwork carried out in 1964 and 1965.[28] Several points of caution, however, are in order if one chooses to work with Rein's analyses. The investigation is centered on work with two Homestead families yet is reported as "Die deutsche Mundart von Amana/Iowa" (the German dialect of Amana, Iowa).[29] A more accurate designation might have been something such as "A Sampling of the Dialects of the Amana Colonies." In addition, Rein was unable to keep abreast of other research in the Colonies, and failed to cite Rettig's 1967 M.A. thesis or 1970 doctoral dissertation when he finally published his findings in 1977. Even so, that does not negate the unparalleled usefulness of Rein's study as a basis of departure for any future dialect studies.

In regard to the existing body of literature on Homestead's dialect, I would like to cite a few comments that illustrate local attitudes toward language. Early in my fieldwork as I was just establishing points of orientation on the map of village dialects, I asked various Homestead contacts whether they would say *Schnoge* or *Schnage* for 'mosquito'. The invariable response was a confident *Schnage,* at times with the self-assured observation that *Schnage* was, after all, the correct form in the German dictionary (actually, it is *die Schnake*). When I asked one resident which term she used for 'jelly', she virtually glowed with enthusiasm as she told me that it was *Schellee,* adding that it was "das französische Wort" (the French word), as though to stress that *Schellee* would surely be the natural choice of cultivated speakers.

West Amana

THE RESIDENTS OF WEST AMANA (founded in 1856) are often called *die Schwaben* 'the Swabians' or, more accurately in terms of prevailing local pronunciation, *die Schwowe.* The term *Schwowesachs* 'Swabian Saxon' is felt to be quite humorous and an apt designation for the mix of origins that has taken place within the Colonies across village lines. In West Amana I encountered a generally southern German speech pattern, though not always specifically the Swabian dialect, with which I have had extended contact. As a resident of a neighboring village pointed out, it is only here that one hears *Obend* or even *Owet* for standard German *Abend* 'evening', a pronunciation that one would indeed expect to hear from a speaker of the Swabian dialect.[30]

Many of the questions that I posed to an admittedly limited representation of speakers from this village produced inconclusive results as far as local dialect characteristics are concerned. Far more work on dialect is needed than could be included in this study. The one point that became absolutely clear was that West Amana is firmly within *Schnoge* territory. A native of this village who has since moved to Homestead reported her awareness of speech differences across village boundaries, noting that anyone from West Amana who tried to speak "correct" German would be looked upon as trying too hard to move away from the local norm and accommodate to the standards of the world without: "Wo ich nach Homestead kam, hab' ich dann, daß ich nicht . . . zu funny sound, [laughter] *schlafen* [gesagt], und meine Schwester, meine älteste Schwester, die sagt immer noch *Schnoge* und *schlofen,* und wenn ich mit derer schwätz, dann sag' ich *mosquitos* [more laughter] . . . das war dann als wenn jemand *Schnage* gesagt habe, das waren [diejenigen] die willen ein bißl mehr sein wie Andere." (When I came to Homestead, then in order not . . . to sound too funny [laughter] I said *schlafen,* and my sister, my oldest sister, she still says *Schnoge* and *schlofen,* and when I talk with her, then I always say *mosquitos* [more laughter] . . . [back home in West Amana] if anyone said *Schnage,* it was those who wanted to be a little more like others [outside our village].) It was clear from context that wanting "to be a little more like others [i.e., outsiders]" was not something one could count on enjoying strong local approbation.

Even though West may have been initially slow to adopt English, the village schools evidently offered early instruction in English, and I have to agree with a longtime resident of West Amana who characterized the German of her village today as having "viel mehr Englisch inzwischen" (much more English intermixed). Although West Amana is not located on a major thoroughfare, it does have a store with a long tradition of serving not only its own residents, but also those from outside including, in much earlier years, local Amerindians. A study needs to be carried out on the local history of West Amana in its relationship to the other villages, and to the world beyond the Colonies.

West Amana has also featured prominently in the humor of the Amana Colonies, a sample of which is shared elsewhere in this study.

High Amana

HIGH AMANA (*Amana vor der Höhe* or simply *Höh',* established 1857) is one of two villages whose speech I studied least. Based on limited conversations, it would appear that the German of this village is characterized by relatively light retraction of the [r]. Unlike the speakers of East Amana, where one also encounters this feature, the individuals from High Amana whom I contacted tended to be "*Schnage*-speakers," rather than "*Schnoge*-speakers." These and other random observations suggest that the speech of this village shares patterns with that of several of the other villages and merits close attention before the limited number of possible sources diminishes further.[31]

From both residents and nonresidents I received the same picture of High Amana: undaunted business-minded individuals unafraid of commercial competition. The reputation no doubt derives from the activities of the High Amana Store (*der Höher Schtohr*), a veritable institution of Colony life. Like the West Amana Store, it invites a monographic study. Fortunately, the tape archive project includes recollections of early incidents concerning the store and its stock-in-goods.

I did not attempt to probe aspects of spiritual history, but did find it striking that the implication was made more than once that both in the period of active inspiration and since, High Amana has provided rather fewer charismatic and administrative leaders of the church than one might expect. Whether this perception is in fact correct or not, it reflects the view of some and, as such, needs to be investigated.

South Amana

THE OTHER VILLAGE whose speech I studied least was South Amana (established 1856). In several respects the linguistic heritage of this village appeared to have much in common with that of Homestead, but perhaps an outsider can more easily dare to say that than might a lifetime resident of either village. The speech of both villages exhibits strong traces of the Hessian heritage, with often individually varying admixtures from the more southern Alemanic territory and from Saxony. Both villages enjoyed early contact outside the Colonies, and both are reported to have been among the earliest centers of settlement to experience the influences of English.[32]

Perhaps even more striking than the linguistic parallels are the similarities in attitude and outlook. As one contact from South Amana put it: "Wir haben gedacht, wir tun's recht . . . wir waren normal, die anderen waren verkehrt." (We thought that we were doing it right . . . we were normal, it was the others who were mixed up.) Another source put it even more succinctly by asserting, "Ich denke, wir sind ganz hübsche Leute" (I think that we are quite beautiful people).

Actually, these last two comments are typical of all seven villages in reflecting local pride and a strong sense of loyalty to proximate spheres of daily contact. Understandings about inclusion in and exclusion from various social circles was—and to an extent still is—signaled by a variety of interactional patterns most fully understood by those for whom such behaviors have become second nature. In this setting no code transmits a more pointed message about the individual than his or her language. At once it establishes and verifies membership in the world of speakers of Kolonie-Deutsch and at the same time places the individual within an understood ordering of that world. As the use of Amana German loses this social semiotic function, other behaviors will take its place. Time alone will tell us what these will be.

Children have always enjoyed a special place in the heart of Amana's residents. Not only were they given special tokens of affection, such as the dollhouse furniture shown here, now on display at the Museum of Amana History, but also instruction in the lore of the Colonies and in the Inspirationist tradition.

William F. Noé

4

Language and Cultural Maintenance

"Mir sind 'rübergechanged." (*We changed over.*)

SEVERAL EXCELLENT ACCOUNTS EXIST of the change from a communitarian to a capitalist society in the Amana Colonies.[1] There is no need to duplicate the information of those studies. What needs to be given here is some indication of the intensity with which older speakers recall, and younger speakers realize, that a change—in fact, *the* Change—has taken place and that there can be no reversion to earlier social or linguistic patterns.

Those who have an active memory of Iowa's 1918 prohibition of public foreign language use find the period at the end of World War I every bit as crucial a turning point as the Change of 1932.[2] Church elders were not allowed to preach in German, and thus services were temporarily interrupted. In the wave of widespread hostility against Germans, Inspirationists wishing to be recognized as conscientious objectors were branded as slackers. One man, too young to have been eligible to serve in World War I but old enough to have known well many who were draft candidates, recalls feeling scorned by any non-Colonists whom he encountered. This, in his opinion, is when the real breakdown of traditional patterns began. A woman of the same generation expressed the idea in German: "Do ist der Bruch [ge]kommen" (that is when the breach came), and added for emphasis, with specific reference to the language prohibition, "do ist der Wolf [ge]kommen" (that is when the wolf came).

Rettig has correctly pointed out that by the 1920s, the youth of the Amana Colonies were restive and ripe for social change of many sorts, including opportunities for greater ease of contact with the English-

speaking world.[3] The demand for cash, rather than simply for a fixed
and modest number of vouchers redeemable at Colony stores, prompted
one young woman to work in the pre-Change era for an Amish family
in Kalona and to sell fancywork or handcraft items to passing motor-
ists, so that she could buy her boyfriend a baseball mitt. Some left the
Colonies in order to seek gainful employment, and apparently more
than a few returned to show what personal, rather than collective,
initiative might achieve. The poem "Ein Gedankenspiel auf der
Wachtstube" tells of such former Amana residents.

> Hier prahlen sie mit ihrem Geld,
> Das sie verdienen in der Welt,
> Und wieviel sie besser haben
> Als unsere Gemeinde Knaben.
>
> (Here they brag about their money
> That they earn in the world
> And [about] how much better they have it
> Than our Community Boys.)

It is generally recognized that already limited Colony resources
were being drained by the many vagrants who took advantage of the
Inspirationists' kindness. One itinerant who asked how he might earn
a meal was told by the kitchen boss that he should go run around the
kitchen building five times. Although no source ever came forth during
an interview with a patently uncharitable reproach of the "hobos and
bums" (usual terms in local parlance), I repeatedly sensed the perception that persons growing up prior to 1932 might have felt that too
much was being done for others, and not enough for them. The tone of
comments shared in interviews seems to confirm Rettig's assessment
that the period immediately prior to the 1932 reorganization was, in
attitude if not necessarily in demonstrative outburst, one of "full-blown
youth rebellion."[4] Although there may be aspects of communalism that
are sorely missed, all agree that the Change was inevitable.

This does not mean that adjustment was easy. Abandonment of the
policy of isolationism meant adjustment to a different economy.
Occupational patterns changed. Wages were initially low, and a poem
dedicated to life in the new Main Office describes the plight of many
who found that they needed—or at least wanted—more income.

Doch spricht man mit dem Bas davon
Dass man ein Zusatz braucht im Lohn
So heisst's in kurze Worte
Mer koennens net afforde
. . . Desswege heisst es zehnmoll
Es giebt kei groessere Payroll!

(Yet if one would speak to the boss
About needing an increase in salary,
The short answer is
We cannot afford it.
. . . So we are told ten times
There won't be a larger payroll!)

Women formerly used to cooking for dozens report having initially planted "gräßlich viel" (terribly much) in their private gardens. One particular woman, married at the time of the Change, recalls the exact menu of the first Sunday dinner that she had to prepare by herself: roast beef, baked potatoes, spinach, and lemon pie. Several who married at this period tell of having received new, "fancy" household furnishings, such as plates with a bluebird motif.

More than one Colonist volunteered a comment on the swift shifting of perspectives that took place between the Change and World War II. By the early to mid-1940s most young men enlisted and served in the military; blossoming local industry was cited for its patriotic efforts; commerce with the outside world was brisk. One might be discreet about where one spoke German, but being German-American was no longer a thorny issue for residents of the Amana Colonies.

Meanwhile some outsiders began to wonder whether the Colonists might not soon go too far in embracing the English language. In June 1951 a person with friends in Amana, but with no specific kinship or church ties, attended the funeral of a man who had lived in one of the villages. Although he understood no German, the outsider felt edified by the service. After the visit he wrote to the head of the Amana Church Society and warned that it "can sometimes happen that those on the inside may fail to recognize a real tradition when they see it" and expressed the hope that the Inspirationists would not "break over to the use of English" for the commemoration of life's most important events.[5]

Today young persons from the Amana area, typically with little fluency in German, have been exposed so often to accounts of the

Change and its aftermath that they sometimes display a remarkably blasé attitude toward the whole matter. The choice to leave the old ways behind was made years ago, including the decision—perhaps at the time merely the tacit assumption—that English was eventually to become the dominant language of the Amana Colonies.

Who's That Knocking at My Door?

BIDIRECTIONAL CONTACT with "the outside" has a long tradition in the Colonies. Tourist interest in Colony life can be traced back to the last decades of the nineteenth century, by which time various commercial considerations had led to the erection of several hotels.[6] In addition to early corporate sales to non-Colonist clients, many village residents willingly offered their goods and services for much-needed cash. One interview subject offered a synopsis of entries from a family record book indicating how many barrels of sauerkraut, pounds of onion seed, and gallons of cut beans were sold during the communal era to "outsiders."

Evidently, those who left communal Amana took particular delight in coming back to show the evidence of their successful adaptation to the cash economy of the outside world. In the poem "Ein Gedankenspiel auf der Wachtstube," already cited in this study, we are told this of the *excolonisten:*

> Sie fühlen sich hier ganz daheim
> Und laden sich von selber ein.
> Hier praheln sie mit ihrem Geld,
> Das sie verdienen in der Welt.
>
> (They feel completely at home here
> And automatically invite themselves over.
> Here they show off the money
> That they earn out in the world.)

Trips out of town for those who continued to live in the Colonies were always an exciting event, especially prior to 1932. Just before Christmas—though at other times as well—Colony residents would board the "Toonerville Trolley" and go to Cedar Rapids for the day. Young women would always be sure to borrow an appropriate hat, lest they fail to make the impression of being fully abreast of the latest fashions.

Hotels were present in the villages even before the Change, and as early as 1933 the first maps of the Colonies were issued and billboards erected. Conscious decisions needed to be made about roadside architecture, and by 1937 the question formally arose as to how far such enterprises should go.[7]

Tourism brought still more outside attention to the value of Amana's unique cultural heritage. It was really only a matter of time until the United States Department of the Interior designated the Colonies a national historic landmark in 1965. Church elders issued a statement in 1968 that sincerely interested visitors were always welcome, if their conduct was not disruptive.[8] By 1976 an article appeared in the *Des Moines Sunday Register* with the thought-provoking and instructive title, "Do Amanans Like Tourists? Yes and No."[9]

One wonders whether today it is the visitor or the Colonist entrepreneur who is disruptive. In addition to tourist attractions of every sort, one can now find or look forward to land development with condominiums, a golf course, in short, much that is admittedly entertaining but has little to do with the Amana tradition. Little Amana, a commercial enterprise at exit 225 of Interstate 80 where some products from the Colonies may be purchased, has become so familiar that some visitors seem to assume that it is one of the actual villages of the Amana Colonies.[10] A recent court ruling has cleared the way for certain kinds of commercial development previously felt to be unthinkable in the heart of the Colonies. One seasoned tourguide, used to dealing with all tastes and preconceived notions of Colony life, says that he looks at the unending cornucopia of offerings to the tastes of the sentimental, the jaded, the curious, and concludes, "Es ist mir ein bißl far out." (It's a little far out to me.)

Fortunately, many tourists do find it worth their while to take advantage of one of the least expensive and most informative attractions available: the Museum of Amana History. In a pleasant atmosphere one can learn what is truly essential about the spiritual heritage and traditional folklife of the seven villages, speak with guides from local families, purchase quality literature, and enjoy an informative and award-winning visual overview of Inspirationist and Colony history. The same tourguide who found some trends going a bit far noted that invariably those who visit the museum like it!

Language and the Church

NOT LONG AFTER the Change of 1932, voices were heard among the church leadership calling for rejuvenation and revitalization on a scale similar to that carried out in the economic life of the community.[11] This rejuvenation included an effort to speak in a language that younger generations fully appreciated, and to stem the rising tide of affiliation with other denominations in the wake of ever more frequent marriages to outsiders. Though some deny it, others affirm with abundant illustrative examples the fact that there was a "lost generation" of Inspirationists who left the Church, particularly in the first two decades after World War II.[12]

By 1948 a nontraditional wedding took place: songs sung before the service included both "Ich liebe dich" in German and "Because" in English.[13] The following decade saw the introduction of various English elements in the service, with the first regular worship services conducted in English in the early 1960s. From that point on, there have existed both a "German Church," known as "die deutsche Versammlung" (the German assembly), and an "English Church." In 1967 the centennial celebration of the death of Inspirationist leader Christian Metz included the reading of several hymns in German, commentaries on Metz's life in English, and Sunday school pupils singing "Faith of Our Fathers."[14] The following year the first *Amana Catechism* appeared in English.[15]

Nowadays there seems to be a good number of young folks at the English services; in the German congregation, there is a single regularly attending teenage member, and his presence is universally acknowledged to be a pleasant but striking exception to the trend. The same may be said of the elder in this assembly who assumed office in his thirties: most of the leadership of the German Church is noticeably older. Of the six elders in the German assembly, many preach the main sermon partly or wholly in English. The only elements of the worship service that will be in German without fail are texts committed to memory (the Creed and the Lord's Prayer) or texts already printed out in German (the *Psalter-Spiel* hymnal, testimonies of the inspired leaders, etc.). How long can this continue? Some claim that the last regularly scheduled service in German will be conducted before the turn of the century, others claim that "the Germans" are tenacious and will hold out much longer. Time alone will tell.

One does hear comments from the attendees of the German-language services that the English Church always gets its way, and "the older [German] people sit there and suffer in silence or ball their fists," perhaps thinking "das haben jetzt wieder mal die Englischen geschafft" (the English pulled that one off again). Some complain that those who are "not of Amana stock" do not understand the foundations of Church heritage, and may fall into the temptation to provide "more entertainment than worship."

Such comments, though not rare, mask the fact that there is remarkable congeniality in the fellowship between the attendees of the German and English congregations. One of the oldest members of the German-language assembly, with whom I have often spoken German, switched to English when we began discussing the Church. It was as though he wanted to be absolutely certain, beyond any doubt, that I understood what he had to say. I asked if the spirit of the Inspirationist faith was still present in its fullness in the English Church, He paused, and then, as though recalling many years of experience and impressions, affirmed in German, "Es ist sonderbar, aber ich glaube es ist, ja." (It is remarkable, but I believe it is, yes.)

Meanwhile, the German language continues to be used in, if not actually perpetuated by, the Church. An elder in the English Church, who admits that he reads the Bible primarily in English, still finds that his private prayer life is usually carried out in German. "Wenn ich morgens im Bette liege und bete, das ist gewöhnlich deutsch, und alsmal wenn ich fertig bin wundere ich mich wie ich ganz durch [ge]kommen bin, daß ich das Ganze hatte aussprechen können." (When I lie in bed in the morning and pray, that is usually in German, and sometimes when I am finished, I marvel how I got through it all, expressing the whole thing in German.) Many members of both the German- and English-language assemblies are active in translating hymns, historical texts, and other documents of the rich Inspirationist heritage, and in 1992 *The Amana Church Hymnal* appeared with hymns and basic documents of the faith in English. Ethnographer/linguist Frank Rehfeldt was able to prepare an excellent scholarly study of language and ritual in the German-language worship service.[16] It may well be that the same Pietist impulses that brought the Inspirationists to Iowa will provide a church setting in which the German language will experience its longest—though by no means perpetual—use in the Amana Colonies.

Perceptions of Ethnicity

APART FROM A FEW formulaic bits of language used to lend the cachet
of authenticity to such things as business enterprise, most Colonists
today would agree—though perhaps not in public—with the assertion
that language is important only if an integral part of one's early
experience, and that "a person who [becomes] interested in ethnic
heritage in later life . . . would not put [emphasis on] the language as
a priority item." A German heritage may be important in promoting
tourism or in generating interest in the relatively recently introduced
Oktoberfest, but not necessarily in prompting intense study or maintenance of the language. Most Colonists think of themselves first as
Americans, like an older woman who claimed that "on a national level
'German-American' is really not more important . . . than simply being
an American citizen" and that she personally "would rather be
identified as a member of the Amana community" than as a transplanted German.

Family Background

PERHAPS THE MOST ENTHUSIASTIC TRACERS of family roots are exactly
those persons who recall being children in the 1940s, when it was
deemed less appropriate to make much of a German background, and
who completed school in the 1950s or early 1960s, when there was not
yet a sweeping sense of pride in ethnic heritage. These are the persons
of the "lost generation" that failed, for the most part, to acquire
Kolonie-Deutsch as a fully natural mode of communication and only
later realized that they had missed an opportunity. The recognition that
an irrevocable transition had taken place left many with a nostalgic
longing for origins, like that of the woman from this generation who
recalled, "Immediately when I [first] set foot on German soil I felt at
home, there was some sort of a feeling, a déjà vu; even though I'd
never been there before, I felt at home." This person saw highway
signs pointing to towns mentioned by parents and grandparents, the
evidence of agricultural and domestic practices perpetuated by her
forebears, and other palpable affirmations of a link between the
ancestral fatherland and her own Amana Colonies. Another recognized
a mill from a piece of popular artwork brought to America by her

ancestors. These women regularly use the German language; many in their generation are, at best, semi-speakers of Kolonie-Deutsch with limited understanding of standard German.[17]

Virtually every person whom I contacted could give fairly detailed information on the town and/or province of family origin. As far as I could determine, most had access to remarkably accurate information. Several had corresponded with or visited kinsfolk including, in some instances, relatives in Saxony (in the former nation of East Germany). Some half a dozen persons shared recollections of having sent packages to German relatives after World War II, of receiving correspondence from the recipients, and of continuing subsequent contact. Invariably, those who enjoyed such experiences are active proponents of language maintenance. Several are involved in genealogical research, and those who can read German, especially the older script, and write the language are much sought after by those who cannot.

Cross-Generational Contact Today

I ASKED ABOUT HALF of my sources what the cut-off ages were, above which one might expect reasonable fluency in Amana German, and below which one could not assume even passive command of the language. The general consensus was that those who were born at or before the time of the "Great Change" of 1932 would readily speak Kolonie-Deutsch, and usually those born during, and especially after, World War II were less likely to do so. Persons born in the 1950s or 1960s might at best have limited fluency. Only rarely would a person younger than this even qualify as a semi-speaker of Amana German.

One does need to be careful, however, in assuming that everything in the distant past was German and conservative, and that everything in the present is American and modern. True, there are verifiable accounts of immigrants who lived half a century in Amana without learning English or of persons who declined to drive an automobile long after the car had become a familiar feature of Colony life. On the other hand, Rettig cites the sentiment of young people in the early 1930s who wanted "to give up the German tongue and be an American community like those about them" and who were "tired of being pointed at as 'odd people'."[18] An individual who is widely regarded as a dedicated conservator of Amana culture admits that, as a young lad, he failed to ask many a germane question of older relatives because "zu derer Zeit hab ich nur spielen wollen" (at that time I just wanted to play). The forces of change have always been present in this and in every other strongly focused ethnic community.

Those whose ages lie between the two cut-off extremes usually seized the initiative to learn English regardless of what their parents may have done or failed to do. Colonists now approaching retirement age often learned English after entering school; if older siblings were present in the home, the language was acquired from those who had already done so.

Persons growing up in the post–World War II era often received instruction from the media. A parent who fully intended to raise a bilingual child recalls,

> My son was . . . I forget now, either one or two years old, I think I'd rather say it was two years and . . . he didn't pay any attention to television except the commercials. He listened to the commercials. And we decided that we were going to teach him German . . . of course, the High German, but German before English so that he'd have a command of it. And at about two just almost on the dot . . . just in one day he started watching the programs, and the next day he answered everything in English. So he picked it all up from television, and it was no more German after that. I mean, he listened to it and understood it, but he didn't speak it and he doesn't have command of it today.

Most maintained active use a bit longer than this youngster. Generally, German continued to be spoken intermittently at least until marriage. Older speakers whose children have married "outside" usually speak with affection of their children-in-law, but note that even if the son-in-law or daughter-in-law enjoys hearing German, the code-switch to English "geht grad' automatic" (just takes place automatically). One woman stated frankly, though with no evident trace of malice, "Wenn wir Besuch [haben] . . . und meine Söhne sind bei uns, dann sprechen wir Deutsch . . . aber sobald die Schwiegertochter drin kommt, dann ist es bums fertig, dann geht's halt ins Englisch." (When we have company . . . and my sons are with us, then we speak German . . . but as soon as the [anglophone] daughter-in-law comes in, then it's all over, and it just switches over to English.)

Many a good-hearted grandparent has tried to speak German with the grandchildren, and the usual response from the child is something like that of one local youngster: "You're talking so funny, Omi!" One grandmother simply admits that when she tried to train her grandchildren in German, they "converted" (!) her to the use of English. Often the grandchildren claim that speaking German is great fun, but "dann weißt du immer noch nicht, ob sie's verstanden haben, dann ist es zu viel Arbeit . . . eine kleine conversation . . . zu auslegen, dann schwätzest du Englisch" (then you still don't know whether they've understood it, and it's too much work . . . to interpret a little conversation, so then you speak English).

Education and the German Language

THE HISTORY OF EDUCATION in the seven villages deserves a separate monographic study, and we can at best offer a sketch of topics meriting the special consideration of future investigators.

For many years the language of all instruction was German. Textbooks were often produced at the Amana print shop, though collections of materials used over the years do include some items obtained from suppliers to German-language (e.g., Lutheran) parochial schools. A division was maintained between the academic *Lehrschule* 'school of instruction', the recreational *Spielstunde* 'play hour', and the practical *Arbeitsschule* 'workschool'. Though technically public, the Amana schools were answerable to a board representing the local population, which consisted virtually altogether of German-speaking Inspirationists.[19]

Local residents whose schooling began prior to the Change of 1932 can still recite lines once committed to rote memorization, for instance, "A, der Aal ist ein Fisch" (A, the eel [begins in German with the letter a] is a fish). Also vividly imprinted in the minds of these former pupils are memories of their teachers, more than one of whom seems to have inspired awe, respect, and trepidation. Not uncommonly, recollections of the classroom include an account of the dreadful *Angst* 'anxiety' felt by many class members, but there are also recurrent expressions of deep and abiding affection and deferential regard for the teachers. A former pupil confided that absolutely everyone in the Colonies knows one retired teacher by her given name but hastened to add, "*Wir* sagen Mrs.!" (*We* [former pupils always] say Mrs.!)

By 1932 young folks may have wanted to use more English; for

older Colonists, the situation was something else altogether. In the
early 1940s, Barbara J. Selzer wrote:

> The older people will never speak English unless they have to. Many
> of the older people, women especially, have never learned English,
> so even today they flee to the shelter of their homes when they are
> approached by an outsider because they don't want to be embarrassed
> by their poor attempt at English. This lack of English is easily
> explainable when we consider that, when my mother was a child, it
> was considered a sin to speak English because it was so "worldly."[20]

Nevertheless, even prior to 1932 English had made its way into the
Colony schools, and several villages felt it necessary to offer a German
summer school with enough instruction in the language to allow pupils
to read the *Psalter-Spiel* hymnal and similar texts with some feeling and
comprehension. In a few cases, contact with German in an educational
context came through the last vestiges of the *Strickschule* 'knitting
school' attended by pupils of both sexes. Such special schools, if still
in operation, were phased out around the time of the Change.

Prior to the Change, high school was available only to those
chosen for eventual professional training. By 1934 Amana had its own
high school, with German as an elective course.[21] In the same year a
plea went out not to embrace the trend to disregard the values of
bilingualism![22] Two former teachers, one who had been active in the
schools from the mid-1920s to the mid-1940s and another who taught
fewer years but during the same period, agreed that this was the era
that saw the change in pupil attitudes toward language, if not always a
change in actual language use.

The change in teacher and parent attitudes did not lag far behind.
Persons who attended Colony schools during the decades after the
Change recall that one of the most "exacting" teachers was a native of
one of the seven villages who was bent on "teaching . . . English from
the word go" and making sure that it was done right! By World War
II and certainly by the 1950s, more and more parents took the initiative
to promote the use of English in the home so that their children would
have the best possibilities for academic success. Ironically, it is the
Colonist from this era who often displays the greatest romantic
attachment to Amana German and frequently tells the most moving
stories about barely being able to wait to get home from college to talk
a bit of Kolonie-Deutsch![23]

A retired secondary teacher, active from the mid-1960s through the early 1980s, found when she entered the profession that "einzelne Schüler" (a few pupils) could speak *some* German, usually because of unusual circumstances demanding greater-than-average interaction with older generations; by the time of her retirement, such youngsters were truly rare. If anything, the pupil who would have entered high school with some knowledge of German might have been that unusual outsider who displays exceptional initiative in attempting to crack the linguistic and cultural code of the new environment. It is also generally conceded that some of the most energetic promoters of cultural maintenance in the Amana area are the teachers who come in from another part of the state or of the nation.

Nowadays if a young person learns German, it is virtually certain to be "bloß Schulfach" (simply a subject in school). If s/he tries to speak German at home, the discrepancies between standard German and Amana German often lead to an embarrassed breakdown in communication. A few youngsters do seize the opportunity that is theirs and acquire functional fluency in Kolonie-Deutsch. I recently observed this in some detail in a Colony native who graduated from high school in the late 1980s. There can, however, be no question about it: this was the exception rather than the rule.

The Amana schools are strong, and a high percentage of graduates pursue training beyond high school. Unfortunately, the job opportunities in the seven villages are limited, especially for those with specialized training. Rettig cites retention figures for 1955–1975 suggesting that one of Amana's finest export products is well-educated young people.[24] The situation in the last decade and a half has not changed. As a result many individuals whose education would prepare them to lend their talents to cultural preservation efforts in the Amana Colonies have since moved elsewhere.

It remains to be seen what impact, if any, the consolidation of schools will have on cultural maintenance in the Amana area. Pupils from the seven villages now complete their secondary studies at Clear Creek/Amana High School in Tiffin, Iowa, some one-dozen–plus miles from the heart of the Colonies. Several pupils from South Amana find it easier to attend Williamsburg High School. Initial impressions of the new arrangement appear to be positive.

Literacy in German: A Dying Art

WHEN THE INSPIRATIONISTS CAME to the United States, they had every intention of remaining a German-speaking presence in this country. Although the *Inspirations-Historie* and manuscript records of the colony contain occasional English terms, the idiom of the texts themselves is clearly that of educated native speakers of German.[25] Virtually everything that was considered important was written down.

The Inspirationists, like many German Pietist sects, cultivated a high respect for the written word. For many years the Colonies supported an active press and bookbindery. Though some influential figures such as Barbara Heinemann Landmann expressed less regard for learning acquired from printed sources, most shared the view of Christian Metz who noted, "Es ist in unserer Zeit viel Begehr bei den Geschwistern nach Bücher[n], welches mich . . . freut." (In our time there is much desire among the brothers and sisters [in faith] for books, which . . . makes me glad.)[26]

During the period when the *Werkzeuge* 'tools' (i.e., God's inspired 'instruments') were still actively revealing the will of the Lord, a trained amanuensis would be present at all times to record pronounced revelations. One source proudly shared stories she had heard from her grandfather, who served as the scribe for the Colonies' last *Werkzeug*. Notes taken by the attending secretary were then written out in German script ("die alte deutsche Schrift"), and the texts printed at periodic intervals. Even during his lifetime Christian Metz saw that much of the extant record was not being preserved and expressed the hope that interest could be sparked—as it was in Gottlieb Scheuner—in preservation and use of precious Inspirationist records.[27]

While the overwhelming majority of the inspired testimonies have appeared in print, many important letters remain unpublished.[28] Anyone wishing to delve into the record must be prepared to read a cursive form not very similar at all to modern European or American handwriting. On the other hand, the copyists who prepared most of the surviving documents were skilled scribes and typically produced highly legible documents. One can only hope that more scholars working in the history of Pietism, German-American ethnicity, and the local history of the Amana Colonies will take note of the extensive collection of manuscripts and microfilms of manuscripts available at the Museum of Amana History.

Those who can now read the German script are envied. Colony

residents who attended local schools prior to the Change learned to read and write it, often as part of a special Saturday school. Even so, as one former pupil put it, there has been no reason to perpetuate the use of the older style of handwriting, and consequently "there are not [even] too many older people left that can interpret the old German script." Unfortunately, German-language education in the Amana Colonies ceased just as it was becoming evident to many that the Latin alphabet and the cursive forms familiar to us today would soon become the common vehicles for transmission of the written German language. The result of all this is twofold. On the one hand, the record of the past is accessible to only a few, such as the staff sent by the Museum of Amana History for training at a special workshop on the German script, held annually in Pennsylvania. On the other hand, because no transition to modern printing and script styles was ever made in Amana's German-language schools, relatively few of those actually schooled in German feel genuinely comfortable reading a modern German book or newspaper.

One speaker claimed, "Ich kann kein deutsches Buch lesen, da kriege ich keinen Sinn daraus." (I cannot read a German book, it doesn't make any sense to me.) In virtually the same breath, she crooned with delight as she told me how much she loved her work translating Inspirationist hymnal and devotional texts, whose German was "viel mehr gefühlsvoll" (much more full of feeling) than the English equivalent. As I tried to probe this seeming discrepancy, I discovered that the sectarian literature was not accessible merely because it was printed in the older printing style, but also because the texts in question were ones virtually memorized as a sacred code by this individual. That, obviously, would not be true of a modern German book or newspaper.

Much the same problem exists for speakers of Kolonie-Deutsch who would like to write in modern idiomatic German. In comments added to her questionnaire, one source stated flatly, "Whatever was taught in our community school during my eight years of attendance, I feel that I was never taught to write fluently in German." This may not have been literally the case, but in terms of abiding communication skills, the statement may not be far amiss.

Some half a dozen sources confided, almost all with evident reticence, that they had taught themselves to write German "in englischen Buchstaben" (with English letters). Such autodidacts find that this is "eine *Arbeit!*" (a chore!). Several shared the fruits of their efforts. The orthography ranged from excellent to passable.

Even speakers who once attended German-language schools often rely more heavily on English than they may realize. One remarkably fluent, older speaker interrupted our conversation in German to spell an unusual name. She seemed perfectly oblivious of the fact that she was spelling the name in English and returned to speaking German as though nothing unusual had taken place.

Others of the same generation may consider Kolonie-Deutsch their first and preferred language, but admit that at least in English they know the rules of grammar and orthography because of the conscious effort required to learn them. Since Amana German is used in rather predictable situations and within familiar circles, it is common for speakers to feel that they have a larger vocabulary in English. Still others seem to share the sentiments of an individual who attended school during the transition from German to English: "I am comfortable using either [language], although I sometimes grope for the right words in either."

Then there is that rarest individual who tries to write just as s/he speaks. One graduate of Amana's German-language schools, who is fond of correspondence and who has written to me in lovely standard German and in charming English, seems also to relish trying her hand at writing Kolonie-Deutsch. I received the distinct impression that she was able to enjoy doing something of this sort specifically because she is already secure in her written command of the other two "official" languages. After one of my visits, she sent along the following note:

> Es war doch so schön Dich widda emal zu sehn am Montag abend, ich hätt nur gerne e bissel mehr mit Dir geschwätzt, awwa es ware doch so viel Leut dort wo auch mit Dir schwätze wollde.
>
> Wo Du des polaroid gementschend hast is ma ingfalle mir hawwe zu me camera "Abnemkaste" gsagt, und da hawwe manche alte Brüder en heiliger respect davor katt, un abnemme is als e grosse Sünd angeguckt worre, deswege sind net so viel alte Bilder hier.
>
> Hoffentlich sehn ma uns doch widda emal, da ma widda Kolonie Deutsch schwätze kenne, ich hab mich arrig "enjoyed" am Montag Abend.

> (It was really so nice to see you again on Monday evening. I would have liked to have talked a bit more with you, but there were so many people there who also wanted to talk with you.
>
> When you mentioned the Polaroid, it occurred to me that we

called the camera the "recording [literally: taking down] box," and many of the older Brothers had a pious respect for the whole matter, and recording [an image] was looked upon as a great sin, and for that reason there are not so many old pictures here.

Hopefully we shall indeed see each other once more, so that we can talk Amana German again. I enjoyed myself on Monday evening very much.)

The same individual agreed to look for texts reflecting the popular culture of the Colonies in the earlier decades of this century and lured me back with a note in delicious Kolonie-Deutsch: "Ich hab auch etwas gfunne wo Dir spass macht, wenn Du widda mol kommst kansdes lese." (I also found something that you will enjoy, when you come back sometime you can read it.) She then signed her name under the highly formal and formulaic closing "Hochachtungsvoll" (With highest respect), just as she might have been taught to do in Amana's German-language schools.

One of the children of this speaker appears to enjoy the mother's facility with words and to have acquired the skills necessary to express a broad spectrum of feelings and impressions in several languages, both orally and in writing. He has even sent me bilingual and trilingual poetry. Yet looking at the Colonies as a whole, this situation is unfortunately the marked exception rather than what one might dare expect to encounter with any frequency.

On the other hand, there is no lack of creative activity in English by Colony residents. The poetry of Glenn H. Wendler, the short prose selections of Marie L. Selzer in her *Hobelspaen*, and the surprisingly sensitive translations of texts from the *Psalter-Spiel* hymnal, to name but a few examples, offer the assurance that the tradition of word-crafting that has been so important over the years in Colony culture has not been lost with the transition from German to English as the dominant language.

"Unter uns gesagt" (Just between us)

DURING INTERVIEW SESSIONS I tried to determine just when a given speaker felt that s/he simply *had* to speak German. As often as not, my question was answered without it even needing to be posed. It seemed that just about every interview subject sensed an urgency to let *someone* hear the story s/he had to tell about Kolonie-Deutsch, and that part of the story was an explanation of situations demanding German, rather than English, as the only viable choice for certain communicative needs.

The accounts that one receives are replete with the usual hesitancies of response and seeming discrepancies of information. Some speakers, for example, do all work with numbers in either one language or the other; some evidently seem to make a distinction (that had not previously occurred to me) between counting, that is, carrying out personal arithmetic tasks, in German and doing calculations, performing mathematical operations whose outcomes are of interest to an outside party, in English. One might tell a confidant how one feels in German, but would discuss health in English because, as one source put it, "All the magazines [with health-related articles] are in English." Some claimed that they dreamed only in German or only in English, others that they couldn't tell, and still others that it depended on what they did just before retiring.

The most important consideration in choice of language, especially for older speakers, appears to be the level of emotional involvement in the conversation. Typical were statements that one would certainly choose to speak German "wo [einem etwas] am Herzen ist" (when something is really on [one's] heart [that is, on one's mind]), be it "gut oder böse" (good or bad), and that "wenn wir . . . aufgeregt werden oder excited, you know . . . da vergessen wir . . . das Englische, und da geht's in Deutsch, dann geht's besser, sieh!" (whenever we . . . become worked up or excited, you know . . . then we forget . . . the English, and then it goes [on] in German, and then it goes better, see!).

German may be the language for expressing strong feelings, but it must be noted that these may be strong feelings of a highly personal and often very private nature. One source, known in village circles for an unabashed willingness to express her opinion, offered a particularly noteworthy response on the questionnaire (see the Appendix). She claimed that she "always" spoke German with her spouse when children were present, but noted in the margin of the questionnaire that this is only true if no outsiders were present and the members of the family were *alone*! Similar sentiments were expressed in a number of ways. Another speaker made a special point of explaining the naturalness of her using German in the presence of her houseplants: German is the appropriate language to express a thought "wenn's etwas intim ist" (when it is something intimate), as when one is in the home, but certainly not the right choice for sharing ideas whenever and wherever privacy cannot be assured.

Anyone familiar with situations in which some individuals are bilingual and some are not knows the dilemma that such circumstances pose. It is a well-nigh irresistible temptation to use an ethnic or minority language to keep a secret from monolinguals of the dominant culture. Often such communication is perfectly banal and may be no business whatsoever of a third party. A speaker of the minority language might want to advise a friend to correct an embarrassing item of clothing or appearance. Prevailing etiquette, on the contrary, proscribes any use of language that arouses suspicions, even if unfounded, that an individual is being talked about behind her/his back. These issues are familiar enough to speakers of Kolonie-Deutsch. What I encountered in the Amana Colonies with unexpected frequency, however, is the sentiment that the ethnic language, associated as it is with more intimate conversations, is simply not even put to befitting and appropriate use in the presence of nonspeakers. For some, this seems to constitute something almost tantamount to a kind of linguistic desecration.

The response to a query intended to evoke information on another topic yielded an intriguing insight into the need for privacy that some Colonists feel enhances, or indeed enables, them to speak German. I had asked one speaker whether she felt that a heightened sense of ethnic pride promotes greater fluency in German. Not necessarily. The speaker claimed unswerving pride in her German heritage, but indicated that some situations simply do not allow her to speak well in German. With curiosity piqued, I asked her to identify these occasions. Giving me the impression that I surely must already know the answer, and speaking with the evident assurance that she expressed the view of many, she said that just being anywhere around nonspeakers of Kolonie-Deutsch made it very difficult or even impossible for her to speak German. More than one source noted in this connection that s/he felt only marginally more comfortable, as a speaker of Kolonie-Deutsch, with speakers of standard German than with monolingual anglophones.

I initially took these accounts of self-consciousness around non-speakers of Kolonie-Deutsch as an expression of the reticence one often experiences in an "exposed situation" where language unmistakably betrays the fact that one comes from a "different" background. Such sentiments are by no means unknown to speakers of Amana German. What I failed initially to grasp, however, is that such exposed situations also make it uncomfortably clear to the speaker of Kolonie-Deutsch that s/he is no longer in an environment in which the choice of Amana German might be natural, appropriate, and even possible. Inevitably, familiar and comfortable environments will become less and less common. At some point in the next century, the last speaker to have acquired Kolonie-Deutsch as the naturally transmitted, preferred language will pass from the scene.

The Still Unwritten Chapter

THE AMANA HYMNAL, the *Psalter-Spiel*, begins with a song commemorating the passing of the old and the beginning of the new. In the recurring cycle of inevitable change, the use of Kolonie-Deutsch as the primary language of the Amana Colonies belongs to that which also must pass with time. The name Amana, taken from a reference in Song of Solomon 4:8, is occasionally rendered by the German equivalent *Bleibtreu* 'remain faithful'.[29] It is my sincere wish for the residents of the Colonies that in the face of change, they will remain faithful to their legacy and choose to preserve the truly essential elements of their unique heritage. It is they, rather than the scholar, who must decide what role language will play in this process.

Results of a Questionnaire Survey

PARTICIPANTS in the tape archive project were asked to complete a questionnaire on language use. Results ranged from carefully prepared, detailed replies, to sketchy and sporadic answers, to total lack of response altogether. The questionnaire is a close kin to survey instruments used in other field linguistic inquiry, and comparisons between the present investigation of Amana German and parallel research projects elsewhere are no doubt inevitable.[1] Several points, however, need to be noted. Because the investigator does not live in the Amana Colonies, extensive follow-up with subjects who have received questionnaires was not always feasible. Since this study never centered primarily on collecting and interpreting quantifiable data, more time was invested in expanding the body of taped interview material than in collecting stray questionnaires.

I have tried wherever possible to include representative questionnaire responses in the larger body of this study. I am reporting here only those answers that can, in fact, be easily quantified, but one may not take the data found here as absolutely accurate. Some questionnaire items went unanswered, others received multiple or ambiguous answers; often the survey participant expressed seemingly contradictory views on a given point. Nevertheless, the responses summarized below are well worth consideration as a complement to material presented elsewhere in the present study and do present a useful *general* overview of language use patterns in the Amana Colonies. It might be worth noting that a nearly identical questionnaire issued in 1981–1982 to twenty-four speakers of comparable ages and demographic background within the Amana Colonies elicited remarkably similar responses.[2]

All parts of the Colonies were represented by the twenty-five speakers who completed questionnaires. Natives or residents primarily of the respective villages were Amana, 5; East, 5; High, 2; Homestead,

2; Middle, 6; South, 4; West, 1. In some cases, "assignment" of a speaker to a single village was not easy. There were thirteen females and twelve males. Five were born in 1900–1909; eight in 1910–1919; six in 1920–1929; three in 1930–1939; two in 1940–1949; one in 1950–1959. All have lived their lives primarily in the Amana Colonies, yet most have traveled abroad, usually in search of family or spiritual roots in the German-speaking countries of Europe.

Because of incomplete or multiple answers, there may be more or fewer than twenty-five responses to a given item. Where I asked for the mark "P" to indicate that a positive response would have been accurate in the past, I have given the "non-P" response first, followed by a slash and the "P" response, as in Speak German Often With Parents 3/4 would mean that three do so now, and four did so in the past. A number appearing by itself means that there were only "non-P" data offered, as in Speak German Sometimes With Children 5 would mean that five such responses were given, none of which made any reference to past patterns of language use.

In addition to the questionnaire, all sources received the "Food for Thought" handout reproduced at the end of this Appendix. Often the interview subjects expressed a strong preference for responding to the queries of that sheet rather than to the seemingly more formal items on the questionnaire. Several individuals expressed open delight at having an opportunity to tell their own story in their own terms.

QUESTIONNAIRE

(All information, especially that of a personal nature, is entirely voluntary.)

Your name: _____

Your place of birth: _____

Your place of residence: _____

Have you ever resided outside the Amana Colonies? If so, where and how long?
_____

Your sex: _____   Your age (approximate): _____

Address: _____ Phone: _____
_____

Your occupation(s): _____

What area(s) in Germany, or the German-speaking countries, did your ancestors come
from? _____
_____

Have you ever visited a German-speaking country? If so, which one, when, for how
long, and why (business, tourism, to trace roots, in the military service, etc.)?
_____
_____

If you did go abroad, did you feel comfortable speaking German? Comments?_____
_____

Do you ever speak German with members of other German-American communities? If
so, with members of which groups? How have you felt about the nature of these
contacts? Did German significantly enhance the communication process?_____
_____
_____

Did you ever have any formal schooling in German? When, where, and for how long?
Do you feel that you have maintained a good deal of this training in your own German?
_____
_____

Are there other aspects of your personal and/or family background that you feel are
noteworthy? _____
_____
_____
_____

Check the box that is most appropriate for you. *If a response was correct in the past,* but no longer pertains to your own situation, *use the letter "P"* in the box that best describes what once was the case.

Do you use German while speaking	always	usually	often	some-times	never	does not apply
1. with parents	2/7	2/3	1	1		2/1
2. with grandparents	0/10	1/3				4/1
3. with spouse daily	1/2	6/1	1	1	5	3
4. with spouse when angry	0/3	6/1	1	1	4	3
5. with spouse when children are present	2/2	1/2	3	3/1	4	8
6. with children	4		4/2	7	4/1	2
7. with children when angry	3	0/1	2	2/1	7/1	4
8. with in-laws	2/4	2/2		4	4	2
9. with older siblings	4	3/1	3	3	2	3
10. with younger siblings	2	2	3	3/1	1/1	7
11. with close relatives	3/1	5	7	6/1		
12. with best friends in public	5	4/1	5	7/1		
13. with best friends in private	6	3/1	8	6/1		
14. with church elder	4/3	1	7	8	1	
15. at work with boss	1/2	0/1	1/1	4/1	2/2	6
16. at work with employee(s)	2/1		3/2	5/2	3/1	2
17. while shopping with sales people		1	1	8/1	7/2	2
18. at religious services and meetings	4/1	3/2	5	9		
19. with doctor	0/1	0/4		2	11	2
20. with neighbors	2	3/3	4	11		
21. with household pets or plants	3	3/1		3/1	4	5

Check the column that is *currently* appropriate for you:

(NOTE: even though we asked specifically for current information, many respondents used the "P" designation (i.e., information given was correct in the past) called for on the preceding page; once again, "P-responses" are separated from the other responses by a slash.)

	always	usually	often	some-times	never	does not apply
1. I read German books of various sorts	1	2	2	11	6	1/1
2. I read German newspapers		0/1	1	5	12	1/1
3. I read the Bible or Psalms in German	5	4	4	9		1/1
4. I use German in my correspondence			2	13	6	1/1
5. I use German with my fellow workers	3/1	1	1	6	4	6/1
6. I pray in German	12	4	1	6		1/1
7. I dream in German	5	2	3	4	2	2/1
8. I curse in German	2	1	1	5	4	5
9. I count in German	5	4	5	9		1
10. I make telephone calls in German	3	4	3	13		1/1
11. I speak to people from other areas of the U.S. in German		2		14	4	2
12. I speak to foreign visitors in German	4	3	3	12		1
13. I discuss local affairs in German	2	4	3	13		3/1
14. I discuss national affairs in German	1	1	1	12	4	2/1
15. I discuss religion in German	5/1	1	1	14		1/1
16. I discuss finances in German	2/1	1	1	10	5	1/1
17. I discuss health in German	1/1	2	2	15		1/1

All things being equal, would you prefer German or English:

German	English	
17	6	for proverbs, sayings, etc.
4	20	to make plans for a trip
20	3	to recall memorable childhood events
12	11	to tell a personal confidant how you feel
7	19	when talking about news in the paper
11	14	to tell a joke
12	7	to make a derogatory comment
12	11	to greet a friend on the street
1	20	to greet a stranger on the street
12	9	to say something intimate
25	3	to say something private in a crowd

(NOTE: some respondents checked more than one choice for a given item.)

Are there any other situations where you have a strong preference for speaking German?

Do you recognize some speakers as more fluent than others? If so, what are the "clues" to fluency that you pay attention to?

How would you rate yourself in terms of fluency (how well you speak, read, and write German?):

What do you perceive to be the main advantages of speaking German: (for yourself, or if you don't consider yourself a fluent speaker, for those who are fluent)

advantage in family life? _____ specify: _____
_____

advantage in Church? _____ specify: _____
_____

advantage in social life? _____ specify: _____
_____

advantage in community? _____ specify: _____
_____

advantage in business or work situations? _____ specify: _____
_____

advantage in other areas: _____
_____
_____

Do you think there are any *disadvantages* of speaking German in the above or other situations?

Area:	Disadvantages:
_____	_____
_____	_____
_____	_____
_____	_____
_____	_____
_____	_____

As you think about your own ethnic heritage, how strongly do you identify yourself as a German-American?

____10____ strongly   ____11____ moderately   ____2____ not at all

Is there a term other than "German-American" which you would prefer to use in describing yourself? If so, what? _____

Can you recall any situations which were so serious, that you felt you simply had to handle them in German or English, even though you would have had the choice of either language? Comments:

Do you feel that someone who has a strong pride in his/her ethnic heritage is more likely to be fluent in the language?
Comments:

Would you prefer to buy from someone who is willing to conduct business in German?
Comments:

Do you feel that the person who is fluent in German is thought of as being "more religious" or somehow in closer contact with the roots of his/her religious heritage?
Comments:

Do you feel that there is any particular status in the community or other social advantage enjoyed by the fluent German speaker?
Comments:

Can you give specific examples of

individual words "only possible in German" that express your moods, feelings, etc.?

German sentence constructions or grammatical patterns that you've spotted in the local Amana **English**?

sayings, proverbs, etc., that you often cite, or that often come to your mind?

names of physical objects or common household terms that you often use or that often come to your mind?

children's lore, rhymes, etc., that you often cite or that often come to your mind?

As you've responded to this questionnaire, have you had any other thoughts or recollections which you feel might help us, which you'd like to share?
Thanks very much!

[A Pre-Interview Handout to All Participants]

In Anticipation of the Interview:
Some Food for Thought

At your interview, what we want most of all is to hear *your story* in German. Here are some possible topics, but feel free to come up with other ones as well. It is just fine to be completely personal and spontaneous.

1) As you think about changing patterns of language use in the Amana Colonies, which area(s) of activity saw the earliest introduction of English? Where did it next appear with some regularity? What are the last areas of language use to make the switch to English?

2) What were the motives for language shift? Were these the same, or different, in the areas of commercial contact, Church life, education, personal lifestyle, etc.?

3) Did all members of a given family tend to adopt English or maintain German with the same zeal? Were there ever differences between patterns of language use within the family, or between family members, in dealing with the "outside world"?

4) Were there certain individuals or groups that you recall as leaders of a movement to adopt English or to maintain German?

5) In which areas of Colony life do you feel German should be maintained if at all possible? In very general terms (speaking not just about language), which areas of Colony life should be maintained without great change, and which areas are ripe for change?

6) Tell us a favorite story or two about characters and/or events from Amana's past. This may be something passed on from others, or something you experienced yourself.

Recht herzlichen Dank!

NOTES

CHAPTER 1

1. For the history of the establishment and settlement of the Amana Colonies, see the first four chapters of Albers, *The Amana People and Their Furniture;* Andelson, "Communalism and Change"; Barthel, *Amana;* Clark, *A Cultural and Historical Geography;* DuVal, *Christian Metz;* Rettig, *Amana Today;* Shambaugh, *Amana: The Community of True Inspiration* and *Amana That Was and Amana That Is.*

2. Whether the Amish are truly trilingual, as is often stated, is a point open to honest debate. Some claim, quite plausibly, that Amish familiarity with (often antiquated) standard German does not constitute true fluency in that language. Exceptions, where present, tend to be based on individual initiative to master standard German. Promising recent studies by Mark L. Louden on this topic include "Covert Prestige and the Role of English in Pennsylvania German Sociolinguistics," a paper delivered to the 1991 Linguistic Society of America Annual Meeting; "The Image of the Old Order Amish: General and Sociolinguistic Stereotypes," forthcoming in the *National Journal of Sociology;* and "Sociolinguistic Registers and Plain Pennsylvania German," a paper delivered in 1991 to the conference, The German Language in America: 1683-1991, sponsored by the Max Kade Institute for German-American Studies at the University of Wisconsin–Madison.

3. It would be instructive to investigate the exact function of formal and informal pronoun use in earlier Amana. It may be that it merely continued the tradition of the German homeland, or it may be (as I suspect) that the expectation, particularly upon the young, to show respect for persons of certain standing within the theocratic society represents an illustration of Basil Bernstein's principle that "every time the child speaks or listens, the social structure is reinforced in him and his social identity shaped." Bernstein, "A Sociolinguistic Approach to Socialization," 473.

4. For a brief comment on this, see DuVal, *Christian Metz,* 222.

5. Sue Goree, "Breaking the Language Barrier," *Willkommen* 11/5(Autumn 1992), 8–9.

6. For Low German in Iowa, see Kehlenbeck, *An Iowa Low German Dialect.* More recent field investigation has been carried out in Iowa, as that by Birgit Rudeloff, University of Kiel. At the time that the manuscript of this study was completed, I had not yet been informed of the final outcome of this more current work on Low German in Iowa.

Often called Low German, though technically something else altogether, is the East

Frisian language in our state. The center of this linguistic community is in and around the area of Butler and Grundy counties. For an earlier account of the East Frisians in the Midwest, including Iowa, see George Schnucker, *Die Ostfriesen in Amerika: Eine illustrierte Geschichte ihrer Kolonien bis zur Gegenwart* (Cleveland: Central Publishing House, 1917).

7. Several subsequent interviews, for example by Jami Fry, have been added to the general collection of taped material at the Museum of Amana History. It was not possible to use these, except in the most general way, in this study.

CHAPTER 2

1. As noted in the first chapter, several studies already exist on Amana German. The approach of these previous works is quite different from the one taken here. Nevertheless, the reader is encouraged to read this chapter, if possible, with access to the existing literature. One succinct but informative article in a popular publication that takes a similar approach to the one found here is Emilie Hoppe, "The Vital Language of the Colonies," *Willkommen* 2/1 (Winter 1983), 1–2.

2. In Moershel, *Homestead als ein Teil Amanas,* one finds a standard German form such as *enthält* 'contains' alongside the locally common form *enthaltet,* where there is not only the absence of vowel mutation but also an analogical reintroduction of the third-person singular ending that is missing in the standard German form. Moershel's work shows the evidence of considerable training in the standard language and yet at the same time many forms that are not prescriptively correct, though common enough in Kolonie-Deutsch: an unmarked dative plural, strong nominative and accusative plural endings on adjectives preceded by a definite article, the use *da* for relative *wo,* and so forth.

3. Barbara Selzer, *A Description of the Amana Dialect,* 101–103.

4. For an introduction to the controversy surrounding use of the camera, see Shambaugh, *Amana: The Community of True Inspiration,* 143–44, and Scheuner, *Inspirations-Historie* (Fortsetzung I. Band, 1900), 473–75, 479–81.

5. As representative a list of early loanwords as any is the sampling of English terms incorporated into the writings of Christian Metz cited by DuVal, *Christian Metz,* 222.

6. See, for instance, a letter written from Liebloos on February 26, 1843, by Peter Trautmann to Christian Metz in Ebenezer, *Altes und Neues,* vol. 2, 55–63. In the postscript to a letter written to Christian Metz in Ebenezer from Engeltal, Germany, dated May 18, 1848, and now owned by the Museum of Amana History, the schoolteacher, Gottfried Mann, notes that he, Christian Döller, and Gottfried Prestele had just begun taking English lessons from a Jew who had lived and traveled widely in the United States for seventeen years. More research is needed on acquisition of, and fluency in, English by early immigrants.

7. Barbara Selzer, *A Description of the Amana Dialect,* 103–108.

8. Ibid., 82.

9. DuVal, *Christian Metz,* 222, offers a representative list of examples.

10. Letter of Christian Metz in Ebenezer to the faithful in Bleibtreu (Amana), 30 August, 1855, in *Altes und Neues,* vol. 2, 377–82, specifically 380.

11. As an aside, one might note that the term *Baas* lives on in the Amana

Colonies. In 1992 the Amana Society opened a commercial garden market, headed by its own Garte Baas (*Gartenbaas*), Charles Hoehnle, an avid horticulturalist who two years earlier had won a record number of blue ribbons at the Iowa State Fair. See Emilie Hoppe, "Amana Commercial Gardens Flourish as Market Opens," *Willkommen* 11/3(1992): 9–10, 17.

12. See Haugen, "The Analysis of Linguistic Borrowing," 90–91, where this principle is illustrated with examples from a number of languages, including Pennsylvania German, where a similar borrowing of *pocketbook* has been documented.

CHAPTER 3

1. I want to thank Carol De Vore for summarizing the pattern that she was able to document through her extensive work with the Amana archives. In a written note she explained, "When last names were used only, usually *-in* was added: die Fels*in* (Mrs. Fels), die Flick*in* (Mrs. Flick). When first and last names were transposed often an *-e* was added: Graf*e* Maria, Fels*e* Annie. Sometimes it was an *-s:* Jung's Annie, Neumann's Rosa. Men's names were also transposed: Graesser Heinrich, Fels*e* Peter, Flick*e* Carl, Pfisterer Jacob, Schaefer Richard. When women's names were transposed, sometimes the married name was used, not always the maiden name."

2. A rich field of investigation awaits someone willing to do research on past and present nicknames. See Emilie Hoppe, "The Gift of a Name," *Willkommen* 9/1(Winter 1990), 11, 14. Several examples with explanations are recorded in Dennis W. Zuber, "Time Touches Amana," which I was able to use at the Museum of Amana History. I am indebted to Clifford Trumpold, Harry Leonhardt, and Art Selzer for more information on this topic, and especially on hobo nicknames, than I could possibly grant proper attention to in this study. For a much shorter list, see Shambaugh, *Amana: The Community of True Inspiration,* 102, and Trumpold, "Hobo Sketches."

3. I am especially indebted to Carl Unglenk for sharing a wealth of pertinent material. Without his help, this chapter would have been much leaner.

4. For excerpts of "Das Sunshine Circle Lied" in German, with an English translation, see Rettig, *Amana Today,* 103–104.

5. Each person was allotted a certain portion of wine from the community, "gemeinschaftlicher Wein," but much was also produced privately, perhaps to satisfy higher levels of consumption by given individuals.

6. Emilie Hoppe recounts this and other local lore in "Let Me Tell You a Story of Amana," *Willkommen* 10/2(Spring 1991), 6–7, 16.

7. For research on the history and settlement patterns of the individual villages, see Keller and Keller, *Culture and Environment,* and the *Amana Colonies Survey Update.* The notes that preface the files for the individual villages in the *Amana Colonies Survey Update* were contributed primarily by Cathy Oehl. Still other information can be gleaned from the newspaper and magazine articles in the vertical files of the Library of the Museum of Amana History. From all these sources and form notes shared by Barbara Hoehnle and Cathy Oehl, I received far more information than can be included in the present work.

8. Rein, *Religiöse Minderheiten als Sprachgemeinschaftsmodelle,* particularly 13–15, 69–114, 193–200, and maps 1 and 2.

9. I am indebted to Janet Zuber for drawing my attention to this consideration.

Zuber has made a valuable contribution to our understanding of Inspirationist history through her translation of Scheuner's *Inspirations-Historie*.

10. DuVal distinguishes between the Swiss who went first to the Armenburg estate in Germany and those who came directly to America, *Christian Metz*, 72, 120. 1900 census data show that 62 of 1,953 individuals living in the Colonies at that time were born in Switzerland, and it is unlikely that at such a late date all were part of the group of Swiss natives that had taken up residence in Germany prior to migrating to America in the mid–nineteenth century; see Shambaugh in Grant, "The Amana Society: Two Views," 6, note 10.

11. There are a number of studies on German dialects that can give the nonspecialist a first set of orientation points in this area of language study. A profitable overview is provided by the essays on individual dialects in Russ, *The Dialects of Modern German;* perhaps less specifically applicable to the present investigation are Keller, *German Dialects,* and Noble, *Modern German Dialects.* All three works provide references for individuals seeking more specialized studies.

12. Attitudes toward Georg Wenker and his work, embodied primarily in the *Deutscher Sprachatlas* (Marburg, 1927–56) have varied over the years. What is indisputable, however, is that no dialectologist of the German language can ignore the basic data and methodological models that he provided. For an overview of the most important work in this tradition and in reaction to it, see Jan Goossens, *Deutsche Dialektologie,* (Berlin and New York: Sammlung Göschen 2205, 1977), Part 3, 110–37, bibliographic articles 50–53, 55, 59, 129.

13. Although the history of all of the villages receives coverage in Scheuner's *Inspirations-Historie,* particular attention is paid at the outset to Amana. One needs to be careful to read beyond the year of a given village's founding, since the inauguration of some local institutions is treated in retrospective summaries, or in connection with similar events in other centers of settlement.

14. Jonathan Andelson of the Anthropology Department at Grinnell College in Grinnell, Iowa, has kindly shared pertinent sections of his draft inventory of residents known to have resided in the Amana Colonies. This information is excellent and deserves publication. My regret is that the data are so full that I could not give them proper consideration within the context of this study.

15. In the Amana Colonies, Saxons seem to be associated with pickles: the local term for a dill pickle is *die Sachsen[ku]kumber* 'the Saxon pickle'. One source suggested that an identification of the source of alcohol as having been "im Sachsenviertel in der Gurkenstraße" was tantamount to saying "right in the heart of Main Amana." Another source thought she recalled hearing the artisan's street in Amana being called both the *Sachsenstraße* and the *Gurkenstraße.* I have not been able to confirm the latter point.

16. For Metz's travels and missionary work, see Du Val, *Christian Metz.*

17. It seems that some of the Inspirationists who first came to the United States (i.e., to the Amana Colonies via Ebenezer, near Buffalo, New York) had roots in Saxony. The nature of any ties that may have existed between earlier and later Saxon immigrants (i.e., those who came in the early 1840s and those who arrived around 1880) merits close investigation. Prof. Andelson's data, cited in note 14, corroborate the idea that the historical questions touched upon here offer the prospect of fruitful investigation.

18. This particular feature is especially widespread throughout much of the Colonies' speaker-population. Although West Amana is frequently identified as a Swabian enclave, the poem about the "Wester Brüder" (West Amana Brothers) discussed

elsewhere in this study includes precisely the verbs *sagen* and *machen* as a rhyme-pair.

19. See, for instance, the material in Keller, *German Dialects;* Noble, *Modern German Dialects;* and Russ, *The Dialects of Modern German.*

20. The record shows that Middle became the home of many Inspirationists who came in a second wave from Ebenezer, New York, in 1864. See Scheuner, *Inspirations-Historie* (German edition), vol. 1, 816, 852–53, for comparative population statistics by individual years for the years before and after the last migration from New York to Iowa, especially the entries for the year 1864, for references to the growth of Middle. For Ebenezer, see Lankes, *The Ebenezer Community* and *The Ebenezer Society.* For general background on settlement, see the opening chapters of Albers, *The Amana People and Their Furniture;* Andelson, "Communalism and Change"; Barthel, *Amana;* Clark, *A Cultural and Historical Geography;* DuVal, *Christian Metz;* Rettig, *Amana Today;* Shambaugh, *Amana: The Community of True Inspiration* and *Amana That Was and Amana That Is.*

I find the suggestion thought-provoking that any negative feelings felt by other Colonists toward residents of Middle may have been colored at a certain point by the fact that this was the only village to vote against the 1932 reorganization.

The centennial celebration of Middle in 1962 brought a plethora of articles, virtually all of which are on file in the Library of the Museum of Amana History. Several were contributed by Ted Heinze, for example, "Middle Is 100 Years Old," *Cedar Rapids Gazette,* July 15, 1962.

21. I am grateful to Barbara S. Hoehnle, Librarian of the Museum of Amana History, for first pointing this out to me, and to Cathy Oehl for providing important documentation on the piece and its production. The title is taken from a traditional Amana hymn by Christian Metz, "Ich sing' ein Lied von dieser Zeit." The program brochure for the 1988 production includes a glossary of local German terms used in the play, including *Aldan.*

22. Letter of Christian Metz to the faithful in Amana, September 28, 1861, in *Altes und Neues,* vol 2., 622–25, specifically 623.

23. See Emilie Hoppe, "A Conversation with Carl Scheuner on Living Life in East Amana," *Willkommen* 11/4(Indian Summer 1992), 8–9, 16.

24. The original plan was to found East Amana in 1859; the event actually took place one year later. For details see Scheuner, *Inspirations-Historie,* February 1859, 636, and February 1860, 666.

25. Rein, *Religiöse Minderheiten als Sprachgemeinschaftsmodelle,* especially 194–200.

26. The pamphlet, *The Amana Village of Homestead Historical Walking/Riding Tour,* though brief, is an excellent introduction to this village and its history. Prepared by the businesses of Homestead, it drew heavily upon the historical expertise of Barbara S. Hoehnle, Librarian at the Museum of Amana History. For the earlier history of Homestead, there is no better introduction than Moershel, *Homestead als ein Teil Amanas.*

27. Selzer, "A Description of the Dialect of Homestead, Iowa." Despite the title of Selzer's thesis, it is a general descriptive study, rather than the specific investigation of dialect features.

28. Rein, *Religiöse Minderheiten als Sprachgemeinschaftsmodelle.*

29. Ibid., 69.

30. The earliest history of this settlement is sketched in Scheuner, *Inspirations-*

Historie, October 9–12, 1856, 576–79.

31. Among the early events of note in the history of this village are the founding of the sawmill, noted in Scheuner, *Inspirations-Historie,* July 19, 1857, and the groundwork for the tannery, Ibid., February 20, 1859.

32. The beginnings of South Amana, like those of West Amana, are recorded in Scheuner, *Inspirations-Historie,* October 9, 1856, 576.

CHAPTER 4

1. See, for instance, the earlier chapters of Albers, *The Amana People and Their Furniture;* Andelson, *Communalism and Change;* Barthel, *Amana;* Rettig, *Amana Today;* Shambaugh, *Amana That Was and Amana That Is.*

2. For Iowa's language prohibition, very possibly the most stringent in the nation at that period, see Nancy Derr, "The Babel Proclamation"; for the impact of this prohibition on another Iowa community, see Webber, *Pella Dutch,* 60–68.

3. Rettig, *Amana Today,* 7–12.

4. Ibid., 7.

5. Letter of June 16, 1951, by C. Woody Thompson to Charles L. Selzer, printed in the *Amana Society Bulletin* 20(June 21, 1951), 1–2.

6. For a bibliography of the accounts of earlier visitors to the Colonies, see Hayden, *Seven American Utopias,* 376. I appreciate the insights shared by Lanny Haldy, Director of the Museum of Amana History, who carried out research on early newspaper coverage of the Amana Colonies. The results of Haldy's inquiry were presented to the 1991 Conference of the International Communal Studies Association, with forthcoming publication in *Communal Studies* under the title "In All the Papers: Newspaper Accounts of Amana, 1867–1932." For hotels, see Shambaugh in Grant, "The Amana Society: Two Views," 7–8, and Shambaugh, *Amana: The Community of True Inspiration,* 95–96.

7. Sculle, "Amana's First Decisions about Roadside Architecture," and Rettig, *Amana Today,* 109–14.

8. Rettig, *Amana Today,* 113–14.

9. Piller, "Do Amanans Like Tourists?"

10. For background on this highly successful business venture, see Rettig, *Amana Today,* 49, 111.

11. See Peter Stuck's comments, cited by Rettig, *Amana Today,* 22.

12. I wish to make it clear that in this section I am reporting personal opinions, and not necessarily the official doctrine or policy of the Amana Church Society.

13. Rettig, *Amana Today,* 57.

14. The entire text of the program brochure is reproduced in Rettig, *Amana Today,* 90–91.

15. Ibid., 63.

16. Rehfeldt, *Der deutschsprachige Gottesdienst.*

17. For the concept of the semi-speaker and the problems associated with evaluating the speech patterns and linguistic behavior of such an individual, see Dorian, "Gathering Language Data in Terminal Speech Communities," "Language Shift in Community and Individual," and "The Problem of the Semi-Speaker."

18. From an article in the *Kansas City Star* of June 28, 1931, cited by Rettig, *Amana Today,* 11.

19. See Shambaugh, *Amana: The Community of True Inspiration*, 198–203.

20. Selzer, *A Description of the Amana Dialect*, 10.

21. Rettig, *Amana Today*, 66.

22. Ibid., 101–102.

23. Dorian, particularly in "Language Shift in Community and Individual," discusses the facts that the tenacious terminal speaker of an obsolescent language will often have experienced a sense of "exile" from the speech community and that a resolute desire to maintain the language is part of a longing to "return" to a time and place in which active language use would be possible. This analysis certainly applies to many Colonists who have studied or worked elsewhere and then attempt to return (either geographically, socially, or psychologically) to the Kolonie-Deutsch-speaking community.

24. Rettig, *Amana Today*, 116–17.

25. Scheuner, *Inspirations-Historie* (German edition), notably for the period after 1842 and especially after 1855. Among the manuscript records, I have worked mostly with the collection entitled *Altes und Neues*, most copies of which have long since disappeared. I wish to thank Arthur Selzer for helping me to gain access to key documents. Use of the archival material of the Colonies has been greatly facilitated for future investigators by Carol De Vore's excellent catalogue of extant resources.

26. Letter written from Amana on February 12, 1860, by Christian Metz to August Koch in Ebenezer, *Altes und Neues* vol. 3, 90–92.

27. See Shambaugh, *Amana: The Community of True Inspiration*, 260–63.

28. The Amana Heritage Society has received a grant from the Iowa Historic Resources Development Program to collate and coordinate the correspondence of Christian Metz (1794–1867). For an early call to do similar work, see Shambaugh, *Amana: The Community of True Inspiration*, 256.

29. The original name of the settlement was, in fact, *Bleibtreu* 'remain true' or (felt by some to express more accurately the intention of early Inspirationist leaders in America) *Glaubtreu* 'believe faithfully'. For a brief period, forms such as "Bleibtreu oder Amana" and "Amana (Bleibtreu)" appeared in the correspondence between the colonies in New York and Iowa.

APPENDIX

1. The most closely related survey instrument was that in Webber, *Pella Dutch*, Appendix A. This in turn is an adaptation of questionnaires found in Dorian, *Language Death*, based on work by E. Glynn Lewis.

2. Webber, "A Sketch of Sociolinguistic Patterns." It is interesting to compare the results presented in this work to those for Gillespie County, Texas, given in overview by Salmons, "Issues in Texas German Language Maintenance and Shift," Table 1, 89. In his table, based on models by Joshua A. Fishman, Salmons presents a taxonomic chart showing levels of language use for certain activities at various historical periods. Although I found myself strongly attracted to the schematic array of Salmons' findings, I decided with regret not to present a comparable table in this work. In the case of Amana German, there were simply too many instances where exceptions and special considerations made it difficult to use such a table without conveying potentially misleading information.

SELECT BIBLIOGRAPHY

Albers, Marjorie K. "Amana Furniture." *The Iowan* 17(1969): 37-43.

_____. *The Amana People and Their Furniture.* Ames: Iowa State University Press, 1990.

_____. *Old Amana Furniture.* Shenandoah, Iowa: Locust House, 1970.

Altenberg, Evelyn P. "Assessing first language vulnerability to attrition." In *First language attrition,* ed. Herbert W. Seliger and Robert M. Vago, 189-206. Cambridge and New York: Cambridge University Press, 1991.

Altes und Neues, vols. 1-7. Ed. Gottlieb Scheuner, 1862-82. Seven bound volumes of copies of letters, reports, tracts, journal entries, etc.; available for use on microfilm at the Museum of Amana History.

The Amana Church Hymnal. Amana: Amana Church Society, 1992.

Amana Colonies Survey Update and Photo Documentation Project: Final Narrative Report. Amana: Museum of Amana History, 1989.

Amana's Centennial Service, Lakeside School, May 1st 1955. Iowa City, Iowa: Woodburn Sound Service, 1955. Phonograph record.

Amana Society Bulletin. A weekly news bulletin published for the Amana community from 1932 to the present; an index for the years 1932 through 1969 is available, as are original and/or microfilm copies of all issues, at the Museum of Amana History.

Andelson, Jonathan G. "Communalism and Change in the Amana Society, 1855-1932." Ph.D. dissertation, University of Michigan, 1974.

_____. "The Double Bind and Social Change in Communal Amana." *Human Relations* 34/2(1981): 111-25.

_____. "The Gift to Be Single: Celibacy and Religous Enthusiasm." *Communal Societies* 5(Fall 1985): 1-32.

_____. "Living the Mean: The Ethos, Practice and Genius of Amana." *Communities* (Winter 1985): 32-38.

_____. "Routinization of Behavior in a Charismatic Leader." *American Ethnologist* 7(1980): 716-33.

_____. "Three Faces of Amana: Architectural Change from Utopian Community to Tourist Attraction." In *Architecture in Cultural Change,* ed. David G. Saile, 45-59. Lawrence: School of Architecture and Urban Design,

University of Kansas, 1986.

_____. "Tradition, Innovation, and Assimilation in Iowa's Amana Colonies." With photographs by John W. Barry. *The Palimpsest* 69/1(Spring 1988): 2–15.

Andelson, Jonathan G. and Marie L. Trumpold. *How it Was in the Community Kitchen.* Middle, Iowa: 1976.

Babb, Laura Longley. "Iowa's Enduring Amana Colonies." *National Geographic Magazine* 148/6(1975): 863–78.

Bach, Marcus. "Amana—The Glory Has Departed." *The Christian Century* (1935): 1083–86.

Barlow, Arthur. *Recollections: The Amana Society's "Great Change."* Published privately, 1971.

Barthel, Diane L. *Amana: From Pietist Sect to American Community.* Lincoln: University of Nebraska Press, 1984.

Bender, Jan E. "The Impact of English on a Low German Dialect in Nebraska." In *Languages in Conflict: Linguistic Acculturation on the Great Plains,* ed. Paul Schach, 77–85.

Bernstein, Basil. "A Sociolinguistic Approach to Socialization; with Some Reference to Educability." In *Directions in Sociolinguistics: The Ethnography of Language,* eds. John J. Gumprez and Dell Hymes, 465–97. New York: Holt, Rinehart and Winston, 1972.

Brooks, Lester. "The Amana Colonies." *Travel-Holiday* 157(June 1982): 4–7.

Carman, D. G. "The Amana Colonies' Change from Communalism to Capitalism in 1932." *Social Sciences Journal* 24/2(1987): 157–67.

Clark, Robert Edwin. "A Cultural and Historical Geography of the Amana Colony, Iowa." Ph.D. dissertation, University of Nebraska-Lincoln, 1975.

A Collection of Traditional Amana Recipes. Homestead, Iowa: Ladies' Auxiliary, Homestead Welfare Club, 1948.

Davis, Darrell H. "Amana: A Study of Occupance." *Economic Geography* 12/3(1936): 217–30.

Dawson, Patricia, and David Hudson, comps. *Iowa History and Culture: A Bibliography of Materials Published between 1952 and 1986.* Ames, Iowa: State Historical Society of Iowa in association with Iowa State University Press, 1989.

Derr, Nancy. "The Babel Proclamation." *The Palimpsest* 60(1979): 98–115.

De Vore, Carol. Index to Computer Listings of Archival Material. [The index was produced in 1991 for the Amana Church Society and Amana History Society.] The printout index is limited to items held by the Amana Church Archives in Middle, Iowa, and in copied form at the Museum of Amana History in Amana, Iowa. Useful for further general research.

Dickel, Martin. "Communal Life in Amana." *Iowa Journal of History and Politics* 59(1961): 83–89.

Dorian, Nancy C. "Gathering Language Data in Terminal Speech Communities." In *The Fergusonian Impact,* vol. 2, *Sociolinguistics and the Sociology of Language,* ed. J. A. Fishman, A. Tabouret-Keller, M. Clyne, Bh. Krishnamurti, and M. Abdulaziz, 555–75. Berlin: Mouton and de Gruyter, 1986.

———, ed. *Investigating obsolescense: Studies in language contraction and death.* Cambridge: Cambridge University Press, 1989.

———. *Language Death. The Life Cycle of a Scottish Gaelic Dialect.* Philadelphia: University of Pennsylvania Press, 1981. Of methodological interest.

———. "Language Shift in Community and Individual: The Phenomenon of the Laggard Semi-Speaker." *International Journal of the Sociology of Language* 25(1980): 85–94.

———. "The Problem of the Semi-Speaker in Language Death." *International Journal of the Sociology of Language* 12(1977): 23–32.

Dow, James R. "Amana Folk Art: Tradition and Creativity among the True Inspirationists of Iowa." In *Papers from the St. Olaf Symposium on German-Americana,* eds. La Vern Rippley and Steven M. Benjamin, 19–30. Morgantown, West Virginia: Department of Foreign Languages, West Virginia University, 1980.

———. "Bezeugung als Sprachereignis bei den Amaniten." In *Akten des 7. Essener Kolloquiums über "Minoritätensprachen / Sprachminoritäten,"* eds. James R. Dow and Thomas Stolz, 153–68. Bochum: N. Brockmeyer, 1991.

———. "Deutsch als Muttersprache in Iowa." In *Deutsch als Muttersprache in den Vereinigten Staaten, Teil I: Der Mittelwesten,* eds. Leopold Auburger, Heinz Kloss, and Heinz Rupp, 91–118. Wiesbaden: Franz Steiner, 1979.

Dow, James R., and Madeline Roemig. "Amana Folk Art and Craftsmanship." *The Palimpsest* 58/2(1977): 55–64.

Dow, James R. and Steven M. Benjamin. "The Iowa-Germans: A Bibliography." In *Papers from the Second Conference on German-Americana in the Eastern United States [1981],* ed. Steven M. Benjamin, 133–55. Radford, Virginia: Radford University, 1984.

Durnbaugh, Donald F. "Eberhard Ludwig Gruber and Johann Adam Gruber: A Father and Son as Early Inspirationist Leaders." *Communal Societies* 4(1984): 150–60.

DuVal, Francis Alan. "Christian Metz, German-American Religious Leader and Pioneer." Ph.D. dissertation, University of Iowa, 1948.

———. "Christian Metz, German-American Religious Leader and Pioneer." In *Culture and Civilization of the German Speaking States,* ed. Karl Odwarka, 54–57. Philadelphia: Iowa Chapter of the American Association of Teachers of German, 1976.

Ely, Richard T. "Study of Religious Communalism." *The Palimpsest* 52/4(1971): 177–97.

Gommermann, Andreas. "Hungarian and American Borrowings in a Twice

Transplanted Fulda Dialect." In *Languages in Conflict: Linguistic Acculturation on the Great Plains,* ed. Paul Schach, 86–93. Lincoln: University of Nebraska Press, 1980.

Grant, H. Roger, ed. "The Amana Society: Two Views." *Annals of Iowa* 43(1975): 1–23. Articles by Bertha M. Shambaugh and Barthinius L. Wick.

Grossman, Walter. "The Origin of the True Inspired of Amana." *Communal Societies* 4(1984): 133–49.

Guide Map: Village of Amana, Historical Walking Tour. Amana: Amana Heritage Society, 1992.

Haldy, Lanny. "In All the Papers: Newspaper Accounts of Amana, 1867–1923." Forthcoming in *Communal Studies.*

Haugen, Einar. "The Analysis of Linguistic Borrowing." In *The Ecology of Language: Essays by Einar Haugen,* ed. Anwar S. Dil, 79–109. Stanford: Stanford University Press, 1972.

_____. *The Norwegian Language in America: A Study in Bilingual Behavior.* Reprint (2 vols. in 1). Bloomington, Indiana, and London: Indiana University Press, 1969. Of possible interest for methodological comparison.

Hayden, Dolores. *Seven American Utopias: The Architecture of Communitarian Socialism, 1790–1975.* Cambridge, Mass.: MIT Press, 1976.

Heinze, Ted W. *Historical Stories of the Amana Colonies.* Privately published by the author, n.d.

Hinds, William A. *American Communities and Cooperative Colonies.* Chicago: Kerr, 1908.

Holloway, Mark. *Heavens on Earth.* New York: Dover, 1966.

Huffines, Marion Lois. "Convergence and Language Death: The Case of Pennsylvania German." In *Zeitschrift für Dialektologie und Linguistik* 64(1989): 17–28.

_____. "The English of the Pennsylvania Germans: A Reflection of Ethnic Affiliation." *The German Quarterly* 57/2(1984): 173–82.

Johnson, Irving Rydell. "A Study of the Amana Dialect." Ph.D. dissertation, University of Iowa, 1935.

Jones, W. H. "From Rags to Raytheon: Socialism Cools Off at Amana." *Business and Social Report* 21(Spring 1977): 70–73.

Kehlenbeck, Alfred P. *An Iowa Low German Dialect,* vol. 10. Greensboro, North Carolina: American Dialect Society, 1948. Of possible comparative/contrastive interest to field linguists.

Kellenberger, Jean, and Barbara Hoehnle. Art and Craft Pamphlet Series: Quilting, Basketmaking, Carpetweaving, Samplers and House Blessings, Utilitarian Woodwork, and Tinsmithing. Amana: Amana Arts Guild, 1982–.

Keller, R. E. *German Dialects: Phonology and Morphology, With Selected*

Texts. Manchester, England: Manchester University Press, 1961.

Keller, Tim, and Genevieve Keller. *Culture and Environment: A Challenge for the Amana Colonies*. Charlottesville, Virginia: Land and Community Associates, 1977. An inventory and plan for the Amana Colonies, Iowa County, prepared for Iowa Division of Historic Preservation in cooperation with the Amana Historic Landmark Committee.

Lankes, Frank James. *The Ebenezer Community of True Inspiration*. Buffalo, New York: Kiesling Publishing Co., 1949.

_____. *The Ebenezer Society*. West Seneca, New York: West Seneca Historical Society, 1963.

Louden, Mark L. "Bilingualism and Diglossia: The Case of Pennsylvania German." *Leuvense Bijdragen* 76/1(1987): 17–36.

_____. "Bilingualism and Syntactic Change in Pennsylvania German." Ph.D. dissertation. Ithaca, New York: Cornell University, 1988.

Luebke, Frederick C. *Bonds of Loyalty: German-Americans and World War I*. DeKalb, Illinois: Northern Illinois University Press, 1974. Of general background interest.

_____. "Legal Restrictions on Foreign Languages in the Great Plains States, 1917–1923." In *Languages in Conflict: Linguistic Acculturation on the Great Plains*, ed. Paul Schach, 1–19. Lincoln, Nebraska: University of Nebraska Press, 1980.

MacClure, Lulu. "Life in Amana." *The Palimpsest* 52/4(1971): 214–22.

Metz, Christian. *Inspirations-Historie oder Auszüge aus den Tagebüchern von Bruder Christian Metz*. (Middle) Amana: Amana Society Print Shop, 1875.

Moershel [elsewhere also: Moerschel], Henry G. "Amana's Heritage." Unpublished article, 1969. Cited in Rettig, *Amana Today*.

_____. *Homestead als ein Teil Amanas*. Unpublished typescript of a monograph prepared on the occasion of the centennial celebration of the Homestead church, 1966. In the Museum of Amana History.

Moore, Frank M. "The Amana Society: Accommodation of Old World Beliefs in a New World Frontier Setting." Ph.D. dissertation. Nashville: Vanderbilt University, 1988.

Mueller, William. "Manna from Amana." *Saturday Evening Post* 259(July–August 1987): 84–86.

Noble, C. A. M. *Modern German Dialects*. American University Studies, Series 1. Germanic Languages and Literatures, vol. 15. New York, Bern and Frankfurt: Peter Lang, 1983.

Noé, Eva Marie. "Amana Christmas." In *Christmas in Iowa*, ed. Clarence Andrews, 55–61. Iowa City: Midwest Heritage Publishing Company, 1979.

Nordhoff, Charles. *The Communistic Societies of the United States*. New York: Dover, 1966.

Noyes, John Humphrey. *History of American Socialism.* New York: Dover, 1966.

Ohrn, Steven G. "Conserving Amana's Folk Arts: A Community Remaining Faithful." *The Palimpsest* 69/1(Spring 1988): 16-33.

_____. *Remaining Faithful: Amana Folk Art in Transition.* Des Moines: Iowa Department of Cultural Affairs, 1988.

Perkins, William Rufus, and Barthinius L. Wick. *History of the Amana Society of True Inspiration.* Iowa City: University of Iowa, 1891. Reprint. Westport, Connecticut: Hyperion Press, 1976.

Petersen, William J. "Amana." *The Palimpsest* 52(April 1971): 223-24.

_____. "Dr. Henry G. Moershel." *The Palimpsest* 52/4(1971): 161-62.

_____, ed. *Life in the Amana Colony.* A special issue of *The Palimpsest* 52/4(1971).

Phillips, Tom, and Mary Phillips. *Amana: Metamorphosis of a Culture.* Cedar Rapids: Kirkwood Community College, 1973.

Piller, Don. "Do Amanans Like Tourists? Yes and No." *Des Moines Sunday Register,* October 17, 1976, 1A, 3A.

Polomé, Edgar C., ed. *Research Guide on Language Change.* Trends in Linguistics, ed. Werner Winter. Studies and Monographs, vol. 48. Berlin and New York: Mouton de Gruyter, 1990.

Prokop, Manfred. *The German Language in Alberta.* Alberta, Canada: University of Alberta Press, 1990. Of possible interest to comparative studies.

Psalter-Spiel, 8th ed. (Middle) Amana: Society Print Shop, 1894. It appeared in many editions; I used the 5th printing of this edition. The original name is *Davidisches Psalter-Spiel der Kinder Zions Sammlung von alten und neuen auserlesenen Geistes-Gesängen: Allen wahren heilsbegierigen Seelen und Säuglingen der Weisheit, denen Gemeinden des HERRN zum gesegneten Genbrauch mit Fleiß zusammen getragen nebst den dazu nöthigen und nützlichen Registern.*

Reed, Carroll E., and Herbert F. Wiese. "Amana German." *American Speech* 32(December 1957): 243-56.

Rehfeldt, Frank. "Der deutschsprachige Gottesdienst der Gemeinschaft der Wahren Inspiration in Amana/Iowa (USA)—eine ethnologische Fallstudie." M.A. thesis, University of Essen, Germany, 1989.

Rein, Kurt. "Deutsche Minderheiten täuferischen Ursprungs im Mittelwesten der USA." In *Deutsch als Muttersprache in den Vereinigten Staaten, Teil I: Der Mittelwesten,* eds. Leopold Auburger, Heinz Kloss, and Heinz Rupp. Wiesbaden: Franz Steiner, 1979, 173-89.

_____. *Religiöse Minderheiten als Sprachgemeinschaftsmodelle: Deutsche Sprachinseln täuferischen Ursprungs in den Vereinigten Staaten von Amerika.* Wiesbaden: Steiner, 1977.

Rettig, Lawrence L. "Amana German Anew." *American Speech* 44(February

1969): 55–66.

_____. *Amana Today: A History of the Amana Colonies from 1932 to the Present*. South Amana: published privately, 1975.

_____. "Grammatical Structures in Amana German." Ph.D. dissertation, University of Iowa, 1970.

_____. "Segmental Phonemes of the Amana Dialect." M.A. thesis, University of Iowa, 1967.

Rice, Millard Milburn. "Eighty-Nine Years of Collective Living." *The Palimpsest* 52/4(1971): 198–213.

Richling, Barnett. "The Amana Society: A History of Change." *The Palimpsest* 58/2(1977): 34–47.

Royale, S. "Utopia in Iowa." *Geographical Magazine* 58(April 1986): 182–87.

Russ, Charles V. J. *The Dialects of Modern German: A Linguistic Survey*. Stanford: Stanford University Press, 1989.

Salmons, Joe. "Issues in Texas German Language Maintenance and Shift." *Monatshefte* 75/3(1983): 187–96.

Schach, Paul, ed. *Languages in Conflict: Linguistic Acculturation on the Great Plains*. Lincoln, Nebraska, and London: University of Nebraska Press, 1980. Of general rather than specific interest to this topic.

Schanz, Joanna E. *Willow Basketry of the Amana Colonies*. Iowa City: Penfield Press, 1986.

Scheuner, Gottlieb. *Inspirations-Historie*. Variable subtitles. Continued by Georg Heinemann. 10 vols., the last 7 vols. numbered 1–7. 1817–1923, with typescript and manuscript continuations through the year 1933. (Middle) Amana: Amana Society Print Shop, 1891–1926.

_____. *Inspirations-Historie*. Variable subtitles. Trans. Janet W. Zuber. 3 vols., 1714–1850. Amana: Amana Church Society, 1977–1987.

Schiff, Henry. "Before and After 1932: A Memoir." *Communal Societies* 4(1984): 161–64.

Schneider, Ulf-Michael. "Die wahren 'Propheten-Kinder': Sprache, Literatur und Wirkung der Inspirierten im 18. Jahrhundert." Ph.D. dissertation, University of Göttingen, Germany, 1992.

Schwartzkopff, Christa. *German Americans: Die sprachliche Assimilation der Deutschen in Wisconsin*. Deutsche Sprache in Europa und Übersee. Berichte und Forschungen 12. *Deutsch als Muttersprache in den Vereinigten Staaten* 3. Stuttgart: Steiner Verlag, 1987. Of possible interest to comparative studies.

Sculle, Keith A. "Amana's First Decisions about Roadside Architecture: An Index of Cultural Change." *Annals of Iowa,* 3d series, 49/6(1988): 462–74.

Seliger, Herbert W., and Robert M. Vago, eds. *First Language Attrition*. Cambridge and New York: Cambridge University Press, 1991.

Selzer, Barbara Jacoline. "A Description of the Amana Dialect of Homestead,

Iowa." M.A. thesis, University of Illinois, 1941.

Selzer, Marie L. *Hobelspaen . . . a collection*. Amana: Hobelspaen Publications, 1985. A collection of reminiscences.

Shambaugh, Bertha M. H. *Amana: The Community of True Inspiration*. Iowa City: State Historical Society of Iowa, 1908; Reprint. Iowa City: Penfield Press, 1988.

———. *Amana That Was and Amana That Is*. Iowa City: State Historical Society of Iowa, 1932; reprint. New York: Arno Press, 1976.

———. "Amana That Was and Amana That Is." *The Palimpsest* 44/3(1963): 91–124.

Shaw, Albert. "Life in the Amana Colony." *The Palimpsest* 52/4(1971): 163–76.

Snyder, Ruth Geraldine. "The Arts and Crafts of the Amana Society." M.A. thesis, University of Iowa, 1949.

Swift, David. "Manna from Amana: What's Better than Down-Home Cooking? Up-Farm Food!" *Mother Earth News* (September–October 1987): 54–57.

Thomason, Sarah Grey, and Terrence Kaufman. *Language Contact, Creolization and Genetic Linguistics*. Berkeley: University of California Press, 1988.

Trumpold, Cliff. "Hobo Sketches by an Amana Station Agent." *The Palimpsest* 70/2(1989): 103–6.

Van Ravenswaay, Charles. *Drawn from Nature: The Botanical Art of Joseph Prestele and His Sons*. Washington, D.C.: Smithsonian Institution Press, 1984.

Webber, Philip E. "Betwixt and Between: The Tension and Dynamics of Language Contact in Iowa's Amana Colonies." In *The German Language in America: 1683–1991*, ed. Joseph C. Salmons. Madison, Wisconsin: The Max Kade Institute, forthcoming.

———. "Crossing Colony Lines: Moves by Two Families from Pella to the Amana Colonies in the 1860s." *The Palimpsest* 73/1(1992): 6–17.

———. "Everyday Elaborations: Three Traditional Iowa Communities." In *Passing Time and Traditions,* ed. Steven Ohrn, 90–101. Ames: Iowa State University Press, 1984.

———. "German & Dutch Ethnic Communities." In *Take This Exit: Rediscovering the Iowa Landscape,* ed. Robert F. Sayre, 138–52. Ames: Iowa State University Press, 1989.

———. *Pella Dutch: The Portrait of a Language and Its Use in One of Iowa's Ethnic Communities*. Ames: Iowa State University Press, 1988. Of comparative methodological interest.

———. "A Sketch of Sociolinguistic Patterns in the Amanas." Paper presented to the 1983 meeting of the Iowa Chapter of the American Association of Teachers of German and to the Iowa Academy of Science.

Willkommen. Edited and published five times a year by Emilie Hoppe to provide cultural and commercial information on the Amana Colonies.

Yambura, Barbara S., with Eunice Willis Bodine. *A Change and a Parting: My Story of Amana*. Ames: Iowa State University Press, 1960.

Zuber, Dennis W. "Time Touches Amana." Unpublished typescript of recollections by the author's grandfather, Henry G. Moershel.

Zuber, Janet W., trans. *Barbara Heinemann Landmann Biography* [and] *E. L. Gruber's Teachings on Divine Inspiration and Other Essays*. (Middle) Amana: Amana Church Society, 1981.

_____. See Scheuner, Gottlieb.

Zug, Joan Liffring, comp. and ed. *The Amanas Yesterday: Seven Communal Villages in Iowa, Historic Photographs 1900/1932*. Amana: The Amana Society, 1975.

INDEX